Performing with Objectives

Newbury House Series:

INNOVATIONS IN FOREIGN LANGUAGE EDUCATION
Howard B. Altman, Series Editor

Performing
with
Objectives

Florence Steiner

Director of Instruction and Developmental Services,

The Glenbrook High Schools,

Glenview, Illinois

NEWBURY HOUSE PUBLISHERS, INC/rowley, massachusetts

NEWBURY HOUSE PUBLISHERS, Inc.

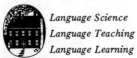

Language Science
Language Teaching
Language Learning

68 Middle Road, Rowley, Massachusetts 01969

ISBN: 912066-89-X (paper)
          912066-98-9 (cloth)

Printed in the U.S.A.   First printing: February, 1975
Cover design by Harry Swanson

PREFACE

Education is on many people's minds today, and it has been for some time. The news media juxtapose stories of educational disasters against educational successes. For every budding scientist who walks through the school door, two vandals, two drug pushers, or two thieves lie in wait—or so many nervous parents have come to believe.

The American dream of achieving success through education has been challenged from within and from without. Too many students fail to succeed in school, and thus get little opportunity to succeed outside of it. Too many students find school baffling, capricious, irrelevant, painful. Too frequently these feelings are caused by an educational system which ignores the needs of the individual learner: what he learns best, how he learns best, what he needs to learn most.

Performance objectives can not solve all of these problems, but their judicious use can and does help to take some of the bafflement, capriciousness, irrelevancy, and pain out of the business of learning. In this book, Florence Steiner suggests the role performance objectives have to play in foreign language learning and teaching. Dr. Steiner's extensive experience as a foreign language teacher, a district foreign language coordinator, and a school administrator for the high schools in Glenview, Illinois, convinced her of the need for teachers to think and act in terms of what students learn and of how students feel about their learning.

This book illustrates ways of developing a performance curriculum for foreign language education. The author offers examples of how foreign language teachers can apply performance objectives to the teaching of listening comprehension, conversation, reading, writing, and culture. She also suggests how performance objectives can play an important role in the individualization of instruction, a phenomenon much on educators' minds today.

This is very much a practitioner's book, written by and for a foreign language classroom teacher. Through an extensive sample of objectives and a thorough discussion of the techniques of writing them and using them, Dr. Steiner has produced a volume which foreign language teachers will find both informative and practical. If learning—not teaching—is "where it's at" in foreign language classrooms today, this book should be "must" reading for foreign language teachers at all levels.

Howard B. Altman
Series Editor

NOTE TO THE READER

Owing to sudden, overwhelming illness and her subsequent death, Dr. Steiner was denied the satisfaction of bringing to this volume the *ultima manus.* Her husband, Grundy Steiner, and their three children, Theresa Steiner Sisk, Frederick William Steiner, and Janet Serena Steiner, therefore, made it a family project to finish the work that had come so near to completion. Their intentions were initially in keeping with Augustus' reputed instructions to the editors of the *Aeneid*: 'Delete, but add nothing.' A few gaps in the thought did emerge, however, and a few illustrative examples were needed, notably in Chapter XIX. At these places, accordingly, the editors have, as discreetly as they could, undertaken to supply what seemed to be required. (In Chapter XIX the missing examples were provided in part by Theresa Steiner Sisk and Grundy Steiner, and in part by a committee from Glenbrook North High School: Deborah Dahms, Julia Guerrero, and Christine Kempf of the Foreign Language Department, and Dr. E. J. Duffy, Principal.) But the changes have been primarily stylistic, and as the volume now stands, it presents (even where most revised) the thought, intent, and as a rule, the very words of Dr. Florence Steiner, whose creation it truly is.

The physical preparation of the text in its earlier stages was done by the late Mrs. Irene Rich, Mrs. Alice Roby, and Mrs. Lori Swift.

(Dr. Steiner would certainly have acknowledged their assistance, as she would the help of the Series Editor, Howard B. Altman, and of the many colleagues, friends, and members of workshops and panels, most of them far too little known by her family, who in discussions helped to shape the substance and argument she phrased here. She would also have wished to express her gratitude to Dr. Forrest S. Sheely, Superintendent of the Glenbrook High Schools, for his counsel and support and, above all, for the freedom to undertake this and her many other creative enterprises.) But, in addition, the editors from the family owe a special debt to Janet Steiner and Amy L. Abrams, who labored long and strenuously to place the last revisions physically in the text, and to Theresa Steiner Sisk who prepared the index. A final, thoughtful reading of the manuscript by the Series Editor capped the efforts of the household to bring a beloved member's work to press.

G. S.
January 1975

CONTENTS

I. RATIONALE

Like most valuable ideas in education, the concept underlying the expression "performance objectives" has appeared at intervals, undergone a measure of implementation, met with some success, and then been swept away by yet another new wave. This very cycle of events has led many an educator to look with concern on any new idea, for he fears another "bandwagon" or another philosophy which will prove to be of no more merit or value than many that have already been tried and rejected. It is my opinion, however, that performance objectives are likely to last, to become an enduring part of our teaching and learning strategies, and to be a major component of educational change in the future. The reason is simple: today emphasis is on *performance,* and that is why I have chosen the title, *Performing with Objectives.* Today's world is a world of action where the old, vague answers will not serve.

Performance objectives appeared on the scene fifty years ago with the "scientific movement in education" in the writings of Franklin Bobbitt (Hoetker, 561). At that point they did not have lasting impact, but they reappeared in the forties and fifties. They have now reappeared in the seventies. Why did they disappear in the first place? And why is there any hope that they will last this time around? I should like to emphasize two factors which help to answer these questions: first, any educational movement must have proponents able to explain to teachers how to implement the ideas of the movement; and, secondly, the time must be ripe for those ideas.

On occasion the proponents of a new idea can become unreasonable in their expectations for its acceptance and implementation. They assume that others will be as easily persuaded as they, and they also assume that others will be equally able and willing to implement new ideas. In order to gain acceptance for their idea they may demand that all previous ways be scrapped immediately and that the new idea have complete and immediate implementation. It is quite possible that something of this sort may have occurred with performance objectives.

Hoetker (1970, pp. 560-61) recounts an incident which exemplifies the importance of the approach proponents take: Some years ago, when he and Alan Engelsman began work on drama curriculum materials, the two met with a group of about thirty English and drama teachers. In this group they encountered a hostility directed towards behavioral objectives, Bloom's *Taxonomy* (Bloom, 1956), and programmed textbooks. Hoetker concluded that this hostility reflected a dislike and distrust of the presenters of the ideas more than of the ideas themselves. These teachers had encountered previous presenters who were "arrogant, badly educated and clearly of the opinion that anyone who could not sit down and write behavioral objectives for his discipline was a fraud and an incompetent" (Hoetker, p. 561). There had been little or no attempt to help teachers learn how to do the task.

Today's situation is quite different. Workshops, publications like those of Robert Mager (1962, 1968), articles and books within the various subject disciplines, programs at professional meetings—all seem designed to help teachers learn how to write objectives. Also, some reasonable proponents of objectives have deemphasized the connection with behaviorist theory and have urged that the objectives be called *performance* objectives since they specify what a person should be able to *do*. In addition, proponents now often admit that we cannot always specify what will actually take place, but rather only what we want to take place. Many proponents are now even willing to accept the idea that some class time can be spent on matters not involved with achieving specific objectives. Perhaps the early proponents of objectives also had these ideas, but those who presented and interpreted the movement to others seem at times to have conveyed a far less reasonable impression.

Ideas that are unsuccessful in one era can, nonetheless, succeed in another. The thirties, as Hoetker remarks, were an age more concerned with processes than with singular objectives, hence objectives did not flourish; in the forties and fifties objectives regained popularity because of such writers as Bloom, Ralph Tyler, and Virgil Herrick. Also during the fifties the efficiency expert and the systems analyst gained popularity in the military and business world as both began to move toward "the cult of efficiency" and toward greater use of objectives.

However, the very acceptance of the idea of performance objectives by the military and industrial sectors was enough to act as a deterrent to "civilian" educators. Teachers like to view themselves as humanists, and they feared that the use of strategies employed by industry and the military would dehumanize education. During the past decade, however, several other events have taken place that have forced teachers to overcome this basic reluctance. Education today, not unlike the military or the business world, finds itself in a fight for funds. It can no longer exist with local support alone; it must receive state and federal funding. In order to obtain funding, educational establishments must submit plans specifying how the funds will be spent. Even local boards of education are increasingly asking schools to set forth objectives when they seek funding for new programs. As teacher salaries have risen, the public has taken a greater interest in the prime objective of teachers—namely, that the student learn. Test scores, rightly or wrongly, are often used to furnish the data on which schools are judged. Teachers and administrators are for the first time less reluctant to tell the public the criteria by which they prefer to be judged, for otherwise they risk being evaluated on inappropriate or invalid data.

State departments of education are also mandating both goals and objectives as they encourage school districts to move to a plan of management-by-objectives or to some form of a Planning Programming Budgeting System (PPBS). Some states have already legislated one or both of these.

To sum up, the past has shown that performance objectives have appeared on the scene, have disappeared, and then reappeared. I think that this time they will remain a vital part of educational planning. The time is ripe for them, and those advocating their use recognize the importance of training and dissemination of information if teachers are to be able to write objectives for their discipline. The purpose of this book is therefore to help foreign language teachers design objectives for their students.

The first step is to define "performance objective". **A performance objective is a statement of what the student can do at some given point in his learning.** The objective is always stated in terms of the learner's performance or behavior.

In brief, a performance objective should state:

1. what the student will do (e.g., Write an essay; Answer five questions orally),
2. under what conditions (e.g., in class without notes, in an individual conference with the teacher),
3. within what time limit (e.g., forty minutes, five minutes, no time limit),
4. to what level of mastery (e.g., must include five pertinent ideas each supported with specific documentation; must have good paragraph and essay construction; must contain no more than three errors of grammar, punctuation, or spelling; four out of five oral answers must be correct in content; no more than three errors in pronunciation).

An example of a performance objective for first-level French might be:

In an individual conference with your teacher you will be assigned one of four topics (your family, the weather, your schedule, or the classroom). Your teacher will ask you five questions orally in French, and you will answer these orally in French and in complete sentences.
Criteria: Four out of five must be correct in content (according to the information you provided your teacher). You should make no more than three errors in pronunciation.

The student knows what he must be able to do if he reads the objective carefully. He must be prepared on all four topics; his answers, where appropriate, must follow the information he has provided the teacher. He knows that pronunciation will be counted, but there is no mention of accent, rhythm, or intonation. The teacher could have included these if he so wished, but he may have felt that at this particular point in the learning process the student would be defeated by too many criteria at one time.

One might ask why it is necessary to tell the student what is expected of him. Teachers might wonder why they should invest time in stating objectives so specifically. One reason is that *students have changed.* They do not accept the dicta of the past, and they have gained a measure of control by forcing changes in requirements and, as a consequence, by controlling to some extent the enrollment picture. Communities, school boards, governing boards, and boards of trustees are changing too. Schools and colleges are also experiencing a greater need for articulation on the national level due to "open access" campuses and "drop outs" or "stop outs." A final consideration is the growing popularity of individualized instruction.

Students are no longer willing to do what the teacher tells them to do unless they know why. They are no longer placated by answers such as, "It will be good for you to know this at some future time." They are not enamored of the idea that because their father or mother learned something they should learn it too. Unlike former generations of students, they do not keep such thoughts to themselves and accept the status quo meekly. Students are quick to tell teachers, parents, and administrators that they see no purpose in what they are studying, that their education is irrelevant and that their classrooms are "joyless and grim places" (Silberman, p. 10). Nor do they stop at saying these things. In many instances they refuse to take a course because they feel it is not relevant or interesting to them, and their failure to take certain courses has caused some schools to experience a reduction in course offerings and/or a curtailment of staff. Students want to know what the course will do for them or what they will be able to do after they have taken it. They do not want to waste their time and money on something that will have little value for them.

Students are also less inclined to take a chance on the unknown. They want to know before they sign up for a course what it entails. They want to know what will be expected of them. Few really want to waste their time studying what they already know. Few want to be plunged into a course that they cannot handle. Performance objectives, however, let the student know early what is expected of him, what he will learn in the course and what he will have to be able to do in order to complete the work successfully.

Students are also less willing to accept "busy work" than they were previously. They will refuse to do exercises A-F if they have already acquired the skills that these exercises are supposed to teach. They do not want to spend hours on assignments that have no purpose or that will not be a part of their evaluation. They want clearcut guidelines to the course and to the evaluation procedures that will be used. Successful teachers are usually those who emphasize what they consider important, what they want the student to be able to do with certain facts, what types of analyses, critiques, syntheses they want the student to construct. It must be admitted that there are also teachers, equally successful, who let students "psych out" their wishes, but this has given certain students an advantage over others. Some of these students are now protesting that they need not be losers in the educational game. They have stated that they never knew the rules of the game in which they have been labeled as failures. They find that they *can* perform when the teacher makes it clear to them what he expects from them. For these students performance objectives are a real asset.

Our society, furthermore, is becoming more mobile. Many youngsters have little chance to graduate from the same school system they entered in first grade. Articulation on a national level becomes more important. It is crucial that the receiving school have some idea of a student's previous accomplishments. If the sending school could forward a list of objectives the student had met in each subject, the student could be placed more accurately, and he would not lose valuable time trying to orient himself in a situation where students have different objectives. And there are frequently problems of articulation even within the same system. With written performance objectives much teacher time could be saved, for if the receiving schools knew what competencies individual youngsters brought with them, they could then do a far more effective job of placement and counseling.

In very recent years we have seen a drop in college enrollments as many students take advantage of the "stop out" and as "dropping out" merely terminates one stage of formal learning. There is a simultaneous rise in *adult* education enrollments as conventional enrollments decrease in some institutions. This points to a new phenomenon: *formal learning is becoming a life-long process.* Failure may even become nonexistent or at worst a momentary experience.

It will not be what a person *did not* learn that will matter but rather what he *did* learn. We will need better records—not just grades, but statements of student competencies. These statements will be similar to what is done with many graduate students as professors attempt to analyze an individual student's learning and achievement and to translate these into recommendations or evaluations. Other factors also support the theory that learning is becoming a life-long process. We see such examinations as the College Level Examination Program of the College Entrance Examination Board; no questions are raised as to where a student has acquired proficiency; if he qualifies by examination he is given credit, and this credit is accepted by many colleges and universities. We also are seeing increasing interest in the "external degree," which is acquired with little or no "on campus" residency; the student simply presents himself at the appropriate time and place for the examinations. As a college education becomes more accessible to all types of students, institutions—both colleges and secondary schools—are being told to take the student where he is, find out what he knows, and take him forward from that point. This implies that schools at all levels need to restructure learning. Performance objectives can help teachers in restructuring.

Students wish to be treated as individuals. As schools and classes grow in size, students feel less and less that they are being treated as individuals. It is impossible to give a student individual consideration by reducing class size when educational costs are rising, when there are more students to be educated, and when money is tight. We have to consider alternatives. Can we use class time more efficiently and yet have more time for the individual student? Can we omit some of the activities in which we have usually engaged, thereby having more time to spend on those which *students* consider important? **Performance objectives provide a process or means by which we can begin the individualization of instruction.** They can also help us within traditional class pacing to provide more individual attention to students. Finally, and most importantly, performance objectives provide a road to curricular revision that can improve both our curriculum and our instruction.

Whatever reason may appeal to you, the topic of performance objectives raises both hope and questions. How can we approach the topic? How can it be applied to language teaching? These are the questions to which we address ourselves in this book.

II. PURPOSES, RESOURCES, and ACTIVITIES

While some teachers may consider performance objectives alien to their work and regard the very expression as technical terminology needing definition, many have implemented performance objectives in the classroom without realizing that they were doing just that. Every time a teacher tells students what they must be able to do on a test, he is setting forth performance objectives of a sort. Teachers are quite familiar with classroom *activities* and tend to think in terms of activities—what will we do in class, or more particularly, what will *I teach* them tomorrow? Will we have a group discussion? Will we spend the time checking homework? Will we go over the dialogue? All of these refer to specific activities. Teachers are often less than sympathetic to statements of philosophy or goals, for they have in the past found them often to be useless. They may have been constructed at the whim or command of the administration either because a committee of parents or evaluators was coming or because the school wished to publish a curriculum guide. The efforts on the part of the administration may have been laudable, but teachers saw little or no value in them. The philosophy or goals never touched *their* lives, never affected *their* teaching. Often they had no hand in designing the goals, and these goals ended up in some closet or desk drawer.

Teachers, nonetheless, have recognized that education needs structure and organization, and they plead for this. They need to know where their subject area fits into the total curriculum. In this day when values are being questioned, when the very existence of courses and even entire subject areas seem to be in doubt, teachers need the reassurance of the value and place of their discipline in the educational picture. Foreign language teachers especially need this. It is the contention of this writer that the proper sequencing of purposes, course objectives, resources, and activities can do much to help both teachers and administrators see the unique role the various disciplines play in the total curriculum, and to assure community members of the need to retain those subjects that have a demonstrated value and worth.

The following definitions will be used throughout this book. While they are not the only valid definitions that might be chosen, they are, it is hoped, clearer than others. In all of them the reader will see that the usual term "goal" has been replaced by "purpose,"and the usual term "course objective" by "performance objective." The definition of performance objectives has been expanded from the definition given in Chapter I. Our list thus includes:

Philosophy Statements of philosophy usually begin with "We believe that. . . ." They are broad statements of a commitment to certain educational principles.

Example: We believe that all students should understand the responsibilities of good citizenship.

Purposes Purposes are philosophical statements, but they are more limited in scope than a school philosophy. They set forth the philosophical basis for the existence of departments, courses or programs, and they should provide a good rationale for the existence of these. Purposes may or may not be stated in specific behavioral terms.

Example: The purpose of the foreign language department is to provide an opportunity for all students to learn about a foreign culture.

The purpose of Spanish I is for the student to learn how to learn a foreign language.

The purpose of Program A is to provide a special curriculum for the slow learner.

(Note that none of these purposes is necessarily the *only* purpose behind the existence of the department, the course or the program. We expect to find *lists* of purposes for each of these areas.)

Performance Objectives There are two basic types of performance objectives: *student performance objectives* and *program objectives*. Chapter XVII deals with program objectives. For the most part we shall deal with student performance objectives in this book. **A student performance objective states what the student will do, under what circumstances he will do it, under what time limit he will work, and to what level of mastery he will perform.** A performance objective measures the outcome of learning. Student performance objectives are divided into two types:

Learning Objectives These objectives measure student performance at some intermediate point in the course: at the end of a class, a lesson, a unit, etc. Each learning objective should lead to some terminal course objective.

Terminal Course Objectives These tell what we wish the student to be able to do at the end of the course. It is by these performances that we differentiate a student with level III competencies from a student with level II competencies. In accomplishing the learning objectives and terminal course objectives students engage in or make use of activities.

Activities These have no value in themselves; they derive their worth insofar as they help the student reach the desired objective. They are usually not formally evaluated, since they exist for the student's learning. The materials a student uses in his learning activities constitute part of the resources.

Resources These include all books, materials, and personnel that the student consults in the learning process.

As was stated above, most teachers spend a good deal of time thinking in terms of *activities:* the planning of lessons, the exercises the students will do in the classroom, the tests and quizzes the teacher will give, the new techniques for teaching their subject, the ways to present the subject more effectively, the ways to motivate the student in the classroom. They also tend to think in terms of *resources:* which textbook to use, which tapes to play, which posters or visuals to display, which workbook or handout to supplement the text, which films and filmstrips to make their subject more colorful. This is indeed natural since activities and resources are emphasized in their education courses and in most of their professional meetings.

One of the purposes of this book is to help teachers take the emphasis away from activities and resources and begin to place it upon purposes and objectives. In the past some teachers have let textbook authors do their thinking for them; they have adopted a text and with it have accepted a philosophy, a methodology, a way of life. They have often placed more emphasis on how they *taught* than on how their students *learned.* To a certain extent this seems natural, since teachers can control their own activities better than they can predict a student's response. This is the same danger that a speaker encounters if he concentrates so much on what he is saying that he fails to note the audience's response. Sometimes teachers become so immersed and involved in a single method of teaching that they cause their students to lose interest in the method, the teacher, and the subject. Methods and textbooks are means to an end—student learning. The range of learning possible in most subjects is very wide, and teachers need to use all their professional judgment and expertise to select those facts, skills, and concepts which students need to know. In order to make these judgments wisely teachers need to determine the purposes of the course, i.e., why the course exists in the first place. Courses may be created for very different reasons, and the name of the course is not always a guarantee of its purpose. How many courses in "composition and conversation," for example, are nothing more than courses in memorizing vocabulary and idioms and in translating sentences from English into the target language?

Course purposes state the reasons why a course exists. Although they do not have to be stated in behavioral terms, course purposes should be realistic; e.g., it *is* realistic to expect the student in his first year of Spanish to come to know and understand the customs of dating in Mexico. Note that a purpose does not state how the student will demonstrate his knowledge!

Course purposes define the responsibility of a course and set the limitations for it. They also provide a philosophical framework for the course and a background for the student performance objectives. In the example stated above, the content responsibility assigned to Spanish I is Mexico, and within that area the specific responsibility is the custom of dating. When teachers begin to implement this course purpose with objectives they will have a firm basis on which to build.

Course purposes should differentiate one course from another. It is not sufficient to state that the student should develop the basic skills of listening, speaking, reading, and writing during the first year, that he should improve these during the second year, that he should add to these during the third year, and refine them during the fourth.

It is impossible to determine what the basic skills are unless the purposes clearly spell them out; for example, during the first year of Spanish the student will learn to ask questions of his classmates and answer questions asked by his classmates and teacher. There is still need to specify clearly how far this responsibility goes, but it is far more realistic than statements such as "conversing with a native on a series of topics."

Although many subjects share common responsibilities, course purposes should differentiate one subject from another. There may be purposes common to more than one course; for example, in both an oral English course and a second-year French course one could state "Students will learn to listen to other students," but the demonstration of the listening could differ radically in the two courses. In the French class the objective might be, "The student will demonstrate his ability to listen to his classmates by summarizing in French what they have previously said." In the English course the student might be asked to summarize, analyze, and interpret what his classmates have said.

The language of course purposes appeals to humanists. In course purposes we express our hopes and aspirations for our students; we state what we truly hope will happen. We may use verbs such as "appreciate," "understand," "grasp the significance of," "recognize," "enjoy," "develop an empathy for," etc. To put it simply, purposes are what each teacher has in his mind and in his heart when he enters the classroom that first day of school. If he is wise, he refines those hopes and dreams and makes them realistic. He knows that all his purposes cannot be accomplished in one year; so he sets forth for himself some purposes that *can* be achieved. One possible list of course purposes for French I states:

The student will:

1. appreciate the family customs of the French;
2. learn how to express himself orally on basic topics such as the weather, family, etc.;
3. learn the basic elements of language study, i.e., how to go about learning a foreign language;
4. understand how French teenagers differ from American teenagers in matters of school and family customs;
5. be able to read simple French prose that is appropriately edited for him;
6. acquire the basic skills, competencies, and attitudes needed to enter and complete French II;

7. acquire an understanding of the French people, language, and culture so that he may want to travel in France.

An examination of these purposes will reveal that they would not be appropriate to a French IV course. This is as it should be. One might argue that if a student had not acquired them previously, these would be good purposes for a higher level course. Nevertheless, these purposes are appropriate to French I. *Your* purposes for *your* students might be different, and that is to be expected. Purposes should depend on the students served, the community's aspirations, the teacher's goals, and the school's philosophy. No one of these should be neglected when teachers write course purposes. Indeed students, parents, other teachers, and administrators should all have some input in the formulation of course purposes.

Course purposes should be sequential. The purposes of French II should not be at variance with the course purposes of French I or French III. In actuality it is a difference in purposes that causes friction in most departments or districts rather than a difference in methodology. Here is where honesty must prevail. Frequently in the past when teachers have attempted to set forth statements of philosophy, they have tried to please too many masters, and in so doing they have promised that which they could not deliver, and they often failed to promise or deliver that which they were capable of doing. Instead of involving others actively, they have written down what they have thought others wanted to see and have kept the statements broad to avoid arguments and to avoid hurting colleagues' feelings. As a result the philosophy had no impact on the classroom. The daily activities of the class were not connected to the broader philosophical premises that the teachers held to be important.

An example might help. Most foreign language teachers have held to a philosophy of teaching the "four skills." In many course goals or purposes one reads statements such as, "The student will converse with a native over a series of topics with nativelike accent, rhythm and intonation." I have seen such a goal listed for a Level I Spanish course. All will agree that this result would be beautiful, if possible, but few Spanish teachers would want themselves to be evaluated by the criterion that every first-year student reach that goal. The more realistic teacher might question whether *any* beginning Spanish student ever reaches that goal at the end of one year. In effect, what is really meant by this purpose is that the student will be able to ask a native speaker certain set questions or will be able to make certain set statements from the dialogues learned. "Converse" implies verbal interaction, and that is where the lack of reality appears in the goal statement. On the other hand some teachers have formulated course purposes such as that given above, while in reality their own courses were centered around grammar, reading, and vocabulary development. These teachers hoped that as a result of these activities their students would learn to converse at some future time, but they did not teach for conversation. However, since the ability to converse is a popular goal in the profession and among administrators and students, they felt they could not omit a statement of this goal, even though they considered it unrealistic for the student at a given level. There are also, at times, goals phrased so vaguely that neither the teacher nor the student understands what is implied.

To sum up: course purposes should be the philosophical basis on which we build our courses. They should be the product of the involvement of students, parents, other teachers, and administrators; they should reflect honesty and should be realistic and understandable. They should assign responsibility to a subject area and to a particular course; they should differentiate one course from another. They should be sequential and should lead the student to the next level of learning.

The specifics against which student achievement and teacher achievement should be measured in a course are provided by performance objectives. These objectives state what the student should be able to do at various points in the course. They do *not* state how many books he needs to have read, how many exercises he should have completed, how many lectures he should have attended, but rather they are statements of what he should be able *to do* as a result of these activities. The emphasis is upon *performance.*

As stated above, there are two types of performance objectives: learning objectives and terminal course objectives. Learning objectives should lead to mastery of the terminal course objectives, and achievement of the terminal course objectives represents an implementation of the course purposes.

Unlike purposes, performance objectives need to be stated with specific, "performance-oriented" verbs. Statements such as "The student should know, learn, appreciate, understand, comprehend, grasp the significance of . . ." are inappropriate. The writer must use verbs such as the following: ". . . *ask* or *answer* twenty questions orally, *write* a one paragraph composition using the present and preterite tenses, *summarize orally* a short conversation, *rewrite* twenty sentences from the present to the preterite." These verbs are specific; the student knows he must ask or answer questions, create the composition, rewrite the sentences. He also knows that he is not being asked to recite dialogues, translate sentences from English to Spanish, or differentiate between the preterite and the imperfect.

A performance objective should:

1. reflect the course purposes;
2. be sufficiently realistic so that all students have a chance of achieving it;
3. be relevant to the interests and needs of the students;
4. be specific enough so that both teacher and student know what is expected;
5. be appropriate to the age, maturity, and learning levels of the student;
6. represent, if possible, the composite thinking of the department.

Performance objectives represent the most appropriate commonality to a group of teachers who teach the same subject. Most teachers would be scandalized at the thought of two teachers of German I in the same school using different texts if their students are to be placed in a common German II class, yet these same teachers may feel it unnecessary to have common objectives. *It little matters what text or method is used if the specific measurable objectives are the same.* As teachers begin to understand this principle they may come to view performance objectives as a liberating and humanizing force rather than as an arbitrary limitation set upon them.

It is appropriate to consider resources and activities at this point. These two subjects are taken together since they are inevitably interwoven in the learning process. Traditionally our norm has been a single teacher with a class of thirty students using one textbook and giving common assignments and common tests, and grading on a single scale. The pattern is still with us and will doubtless continue in many classroom situations. There is, however, a wave of change sweeping across the country. The world of resources is changing as rapidly as our student population. We must locate and utilize a much wider range of books, tapes, films, and workbooks than we have in the past. We must select a variety of different materials that will help students reach a common objective since we have to recognize and deal with the various learning styles that students have developed. As our student population changes in foreign language classes, so, too, must our materials change. We must select some materials for the poor reader, others for the gifted one. Instead of embracing a single set of materials, the foreign language teacher of the future will need to become an expert on available materials. Meeting student interests will become a prime concern as we select a variety of resources, and we will select these resources to help us meet our objectives.

The concept of class activities will change both for group-paced classes and for classes on individualized learning. Class activities will no longer involve rote following of materials in a single text or set of materials. Teachers will select and plan activities which in their opinion will best help students meet their performance objectives. Teacher presentations and homework assignments may or may not follow the text. Teachers will ask themselves, "What activities, exercises or tasks do I think will best help Student A be able to perform what is stated in the objective?" Teachers will then select and advise the student to do those activities that will help *him;* as a result the student will see the reason for engaging in the activities since he will know in advance what objectives he must meet.

As teachers become oriented to this "new" way of teaching, they will find that the ordering of purposes, performance objectives, resources, and activities is a logical sequence. They will feel more secure in the selection of materials and in the choice of class activities. They will be able more comfortably to answer the question, "Why do we teach foreign languages?", and they will have the support of students, parents, other teachers, and administrators. They will be able more easily to defend what they are doing.

Summary

Purposes state the *whys* of the course—why the course exists.

Performance objectives state the *what* of the course—what the student can do as a result of the learning.

Activities are the *exercises* that the student undertakes in order to learn. They are what the student does with the resources at his disposal.

Resources are the *material and personnel* that the student works with in order to learn.

III. APPROACHES TO SELECTING OBJECTIVES

Once a teacher or team of teachers has decided to write performance objectives for a course, the question arises immediately of where to begin. Should one begin where one is? Should a teacher base his performance objectives on the text he is currently using? Should he begin with the school philosophy, and, if so, what does he do if the school has no expressed philosophy? I should like to suggest that there are at least three approaches that have been used by various groups, each approach with advantages and disadvantages. At the risk of oversimplification, I have assigned labels to these approaches: the first can be called the *conversion system:* in this approach a teacher converts the book or set of materials he is using into performance terms. The second I have called the *adaptive system:* with this approach a teacher adapts his own system and materials into a performance curriculum; he does not follow a single text but may rearrange a text, supplement it with other materials, select and retain portions of it, and delete other portions; in short, the teacher utilizes a modified eclectic approach. The third approach can be called the *goal refinement system:* with this approach a teacher begins with the school philosophy, breaks it down into subgoals, refines the subgoals into purposes, and further refines the

Materials in this chapter were derived in part from the *1971 ACTFL Symposium on Performance Objectives* (see Jenks, *et al.,* 1972). Thanks are owed to the Far West Laboratory and to ACTFL for permission to use these materials.

purposes into performance objectives. The labels for the first two approaches are my own; the goal refinement system was discussed in the 1971 ACTFL Symposium on Performance Objectives held in Chicago, Illinois.

In my opinion the goal refinement system yields the best and most lasting results. Nevertheless, pressures from administrators, school boards, state offices, etc. may not allow the necessary time to utilize this approach, for this system is by far the most time-consuming. It is also possible that teachers will feel more secure if they can start with what they know—their current texts and their current practices. Let us therefore consider the first two systems for developing a performance curriculum.

Acquiring a different point of view or a different set of habits is not easy. We all like to begin where we are. Teachers tend to think of curriculum in terms of texts or single sets of materials since they believe that textbook authors and publishers have studied the materials, have surveyed the field, have adopted a particular philosophy, and have selected the best materials and best activities possible. This is actually what most textbook authors and their publishers try to do. But unfortunately most authors and publishers are writing for the "average" class, for the "typical" class, and no single class is ever average or typical. It is also impossible to write a single text that meets the needs of all students. Nevertheless, if anyone adopts the conversion system, he must examine the materials from the author's as well as from his own point of view. He must ask:

1. What did the author hope that the student would be able to do after he had completed these exercises?
2. How much of the material did the author expect the student to master for active use and how much for passive use?
3. What do I think the student should be able to do at the end of this unit? This lesson?
4. How much material do I feel that the student should master for active use?

One good way to answer these questions is to examine any tests furnished by the publishers. These tests may point out significant desired behaviors. The teacher should also look at any tests based on this material that he himself has made. What he has put into his own test is probably what he considers most important for the student to know.

Next, look at the dialogues, the vocabulary, the structures included in the lesson. The teacher should ask himself, "How much of this must the *average* student, or every student in the class, master before going to the next lesson? Which of the basic sentences, the vocabulary words or idioms, and the structures are absolutely essential for every student in the class? What should each student be able to do with these sentences, words, or structures?"

It is advisable at this point to make a list of these sentences, words, and structures. Then one should list what the student should be able to do with each of these and with any other material in the chapter that is to be learned. Do not forget the oral part of your test. Is there a listening comprehension section? Is there a passage to be read aloud? Is there a section to which the student must respond orally? Put it down on paper.

Next, consider the amount of time that you wish to spend on the unit or lesson. Remember that if you ask students to *master* material this will take longer than simply becoming familiar with it. It does make a difference whether vocabulary will be tested from English to French as follows:

Give the French for the following:

1. the house _____
2. the dog _____
3. the airplane_____

or in this manner:

Select the correct meaning for each English word given:

1. (the house)   1. *le chien,* 2. *l'avion,* 3. *la maison,*

or like this:

Choisissez la définition qui convient:

1. *une maison*
   1. *genre de mammiféres carnivores digitigrades généralment réduit en domesticité*
   2. *construction destinée à l'habitation humaine*
   3. *appareil de navigation aérienne*

or under these conditions:

> Use the following words in a French sentence in such a way that you demonstrate that you know the meaning of each: *la maison, le chien, l'avion.*

Each of the above testing devices examines in some way the student's knowledge of the meaning of the three words. There is, however, a world of difference among the various testing devices. The second one is obviously the easiest since the student simply has to recognize the word; he does not have to spell it correctly, nor does he have to understand a long definition in French. There may be times when, in the teacher's opinion, a word is of little importance. Nevertheless, if this word is important to the textbook author, it may turn up as a key word in the next chapter. When a teacher uses the conversion system, he must be very careful to determine how the author deals with vocabulary, dialogues, and structures.

One must also keep *feasibility* in mind. Many teachers claim that each student ought to know everything in a chapter, yet teachers realistically cannot operate on this principle. They may have to pass students who have not *mastered* anything in a chapter but who have gleaned a smattering of structure, vocabulary, or reading ability. The conversion method enables the teacher to point out to the student *before* he begins a lesson or a unit the principle points, the most important things to be learned, and the performance on which he will be graded. The student then can aim for these targets. He will learn other things as well, to be sure, but he will be approaching the chapter with much more confidence, since he knows what is expected of him.

The conversion system is relatively simple since teachers can divide the work by chapters and each can write objectives for a certain number of chapters. They do not need to worry about sequencing if the book itself is properly sequenced, but, if it is not, this can present a serious problem. Many teachers have discovered, moreover, that the authors do not always make clear what structures, what vocabulary, or what basic sentences are important, and that some texts do not differentiate between active and passive vocabulary. Some dialogues are so seeded with different structures that it is impossible to master all of them. These are flaws which the teacher may not have noticed previously. He may not have checked to see where there were points of re-entry (i.e., re-use of vocabulary or principles earlier employed). *The conversion system helps the teacher gain a better perspective on the text or materials that he is teaching.* It may not, however, help him solve all the problems which can result from adhering strictly to one text.

To sum up, the conversion system offers the following advantages:

1. Content is easy to control since it should already be sequenced in the text materials.
2. Exercises, drill material, and tapes most likely exist and are at hand.
3. Several teachers can divide up the work if each takes different chapters.
4. It is an easy way to begin since teachers understand textbooks better than performance objectives.
5. It is less time-consuming; it can be readily completed and provides one with something in hand.
6. It provides a better perspective for evaluating a particular text and also for evaluating future texts.
7. It is less costly than other systems.

There are additional advantages as well. Some publishers are now beginning to publish performance objectives with their texts. This gives teachers an opportunity to see what the authors expect students to be able to do at the end of the time spent studying the text.

This system does, nevertheless, have its disadvantages:

1. First, the philosophy of the teachers and the philosophy of the textbook authors must be the same, or the teacher will be pulled in two directions. This frequently happens when a teacher is forced to use a text with which he is in disagreement.
2. If a change of textbook occurs, much of the teacher's good work is useless unless the new text closely resembles the former text.
3. The materials dictate the format of the course; the teacher's or district philosophy have less influence over the structure of the course.
4. This system makes no provision for articulation with systems that use different texts.
5. This system does not allow proper latitude for selecting the best materials to meet the individual student's needs.

If the materials are one-dimensional in the first place, the objectives will point up their limitations and accentuate them; this effect could be an advantage if it results in a decision to change the curriculum in some way. The decision is up to you. You may select the conversion system as your first step, or you may prefer to consider the adaptive system, which resembles the conversion system but leaves much more latitude and freedom and hence much more work for the teacher.

If a teacher feels a need to supplement the basic text to achieve his goals, he may choose the adaptive approach to performance objectives. This teacher normally uses a single text or set of materials as a main resource, but he also uses films, tapes, poems, newspapers, handouts, or workbooks from other sources. He may even write some of his own materials. Such a teacher has already elected to go the performance objective route even though he may not realize it. By supplementing the basic text with other materials, he is implying that the textbook publisher's objectives do not meet all the needs of all his students. Just as he adapts the text and supplementary materials to his own needs and to those of his students, he will select, write or adapt performance objectives which reflect these needs but which are based on the materials he is currently using. There are some basic rules which a teacher should follow if he chooses this system:

1. He should begin by examining the materials he is currently teaching, whatever their origin: for example, the basic text, a reader, and various records, tapes, and films which may or may not have been designed to accompany the basic text he is using.

2. He should elect to do only a small amount of curriculum revision at the time of constructing his performance objectives, since he knows that major curriculum revision will take too much time from the project.

3. He should secure input from students, parents, and other teachers and should then write course purposes. Since he may view teaching from the text differently from his colleagues he needs to be sure that his work will be accepted by those around him. If his purposes are accepted by the other teachers, by students, and by parents he has a firm basis for writing his objectives.

4. He should put the text aside as he writes his purposes and terminal course objectives: he should use the text for writing learning objectives and for sequencing these objectives.

5. If possible, he should try to involve a team of teachers in the project so that the work will not be overwhelming and so that his objectives may also reflect the thinking of his colleagues.

The most difficult step may be to secure agreement on the course purposes. Once these have been defined, even imperfectly, the next step can be taken, namely, to determine what students should be able to do at the end of the course. Here the teacher must be realistic and think of *all* his students, not only the brightest. It might be advisable to have a teacher of the next level up sit in on this session. That person ought to know what students need to be able to do to perform successfully upon entering the next level. Once the teacher knows what his students should be able to do at the end of the course, he is now ready to begin writing his learning objectives.

This is the place where he should take the basic text, chapter by chapter, and see how it meets his terminal course objectives. If he feels that the text provides material for many points that are not covered by his objectives, he has two choices: either to delete those parts of the text or to add to his objectives so that there are objectives that cover all the materials. Most teachers are used to deleting portions of a text, so this choice will be a natural one. If the teacher has objectives that cannot be implemented by the materials in the text he must add materials from other sources that will help his students reach the objectives. Now let me add a word of caution: in a performance curriculum, it is much easier to add outside content to an existing text than it is to risk deleting from it. Yet here again, one must order priorities and decide what is most important for students to learn. Terminal course objectives will be of no value if they are not realistic. This is the point where the teacher becomes an "architect of learning." He determines to what extent his text is compatible with his terminal objectives, and this gives him a much firmer basis for approaching the administration for funds to purchase additional materials to supplement his program.

The writing of learning objectives is easy once the terminal course objectives have been well defined. As he writes his learning objectives the teacher asks himself, "What are the smaller steps of learning that lead to larger segments of learning?" One of his terminal course objectives might be:

> When presented with a paragraph of simple edited prose the student will ask orally five questions using the words "who," "what," "why," "when," and "how"; he may limit himself to the present tense in three questions, but he must use a preterite in two of the questions.

If the teacher were writing a learning objective to implement this terminal course objective he might ask the student to do the following:

Turn the following five sentences into questions using the words, "who," "what," "where," "when":

The book is on the table.
Mary is going to the market at ten o'clock.
The train arrived at the station before noon.
We gave the book to John yesterday.
He saw Pedro at the movies last night.

Notice that this objective is much more limited. The student may be asked to do this objective in writing; he may then be asked to do it orally. Obviously, there are no conditions, time limits, or criteria given here, and these certainly need to be added. Learning objectives, however, are smaller, more manageable objectives that build the various skills and competencies needed for the terminal course objectives. Frequently the content is *provided* the student in advance, and if not, content coverage is always *indicated.*

The teacher needs also to prepare a list of activities to help the students reach the objective. The list might look like this:

1. Read the passage on page 18.
2. Study the questions on page 19 and prepare oral answers to them.
3. Study the handout on formulating questions.
4. Compose two questions each using "Who," "what," "where" that do not appear in the questions on page 19.
5. Participate in your conversation group by asking your classmates these questions.
6. Prepare in writing all the questions you could ask using "who," "what," or "where" for the five statements in the objective. Check these with the teacher.
7. Without using what you proposed in (6), ask the people in your conversation group "who," "what," or "where" questions.

Notice that not all these activities may be appropriate for all students. If a student can already do activity (7), the teacher may not want to ask him to do any of the others, but that is the teacher's decision.

Advantages of the Adaptive System
1. Teachers make the curricular decisions instead of leaving them to

publishers or textbook authors.

2. All class activities are aimed at helping the students achieve those objectives that their *teachers* feel are important.

3. There is room for some curricular revision since teachers are now deleting from or adding to a single text.

4. Teachers start from what they are currently doing, or, if not, they work in a small area of "the unknown."

5. Teachers have a philosophical premise on which to build the course objectives.

6. The plan can be implemented gradually.

7. The process is a good step towards individualization since teachers see students working with multiple resources and multiple activities.

8. If teachers later decide to change texts, their work will be pertinent to the next text since it will not be based solely upon one set of materials.

9. Teachers will have a better knowledge of the text they are currently using and will know what to look for when they select other texts.

Disadvantages of the Adaptive System

1. One is tempted to engage in too much curriculum reform and not get the job done.

2. It requires *time* to discuss common purposes and objectives and to reach agreement. (This time is usually well spent!)

3. Some teachers are put off balance by using materials from more than one source.

4. Since it is difficult to omit content from a sequenced text, one is tempted to include everything and make the objectives unrealistic.

The adaptive method is a halfway stage between the conversion and the goal refinement systems. It is for those who want to try a new process but are not ready to go the entire route. It is a good place to begin because it opens the door to curriculum revision, to articulation discussions, to textbook selection, and to pupil evaluation.

For those who do choose to go the entire route, the most difficult but also the most rewarding process of writing performance objectives is the goal refinement system. In this approach teachers begin by considering the district or school philosophy and refine it into goals, departmental purposes, course purposes, terminal course objectives, and learning objectives.

A school philosophy is a statement of general beliefs. These are usually listed in a few paragraphs and comprise the philosophical platform of the school. In order to implement this philosophy it is important for the staff to break it down, i.e., to refine it into more specific goals. In some instances, a single plank of the platform may in itself state the goal. The attainment of these goals should result in the realization of the school's philosophy. Most goals are general enough that responsibility for their attainment belongs to several departments or areas of the school. Sometimes these areas do not all accept the responsibility for the attainment of a goal. An example is the "ability to communicate effectively orally and in writing." Many school people would assign this goal exclusively to the English department; in some schools the English faculty may not accept this as their mission; in others the faculty may feel that it is of secondary importance to the teaching of literature; in still others the department may feel that it shares this responsibility with the entire school staff. When we refine the philosophy into goals, and when certain departments are assigned the responsibility for each goal, this type of disagreement should disappear.

Each department of the school should then turn to its stated purposes, its reasons for existing. These purposes should be consistent and compatible with the school goals and hence with the school philosophy. The realization of the departmental purposes should help attain the school goals; there should be no departmental purpose that does not serve some goal, and no goal should be poorly served by having too few departmental purposes.

Specific course purposes should now implement the departmental purposes. These specific course purposes should show the responsibility assigned to a given level of learning. These purposes are refined into terminal course objectives which indicate what a student should be able to do at the end of the course. All these objectives will be consistent and compatible with the district philosophy if the goal refinement system is utilized. The opposite page shows how this process might look in chart form.

From this chart it is clear that various departments have responsibility and are accountable for Goal III. I have illustrated only the foreign language department's development of a single goal. Notice that only a portion of courses may contribute to the realization of a single goal, and each department may have

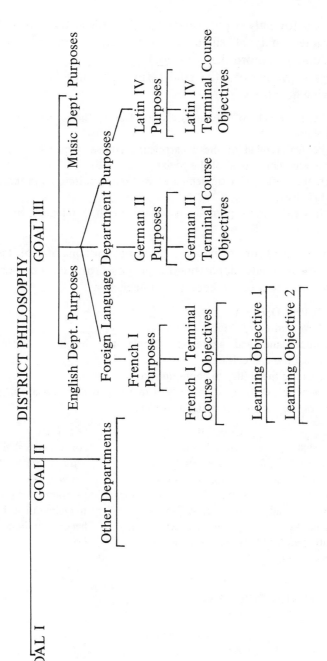

responsibility for only a portion of the district's goals. It is of course also possible that a single course may contribute to the accomplishment of more than one goal.

Teachers working with the goal refinement method need to ask the following questions:

1. Will the attainment of all the goals best lead to the realization of the school's philosophy?
2. Will the achievement of the departmental course purposes listed best lead to the accomplishment of the goals?
3. Is each goal sufficiently implemented by course purposes and terminal course objectives?
4. Is each set of course purposes necessary for the attainment of some goal?

It might be appropriate here to examine portions of a philosophy together with its goals, departmental purposes, and course objectives to see how this process can become operative:

DISTRICT PHILOSOPHY
    We believe that every student should
        . . .understand and appreciate people who belong to different nationalities and cultures.
        . . .acquire the ability to communicate with others.
        . . .acquire an ability to learn how to learn so that he can function successfully in an ever-changing society.

GOAL I	GOAL II	GOAL III
All students shall acquire sufficient knowledge, skills, and attitudes to help them understand, appreciate, and live together with peoples different from themselves.	All students shall develop sufficient communications skills to be able to communicate in depth with those people with whom they come into contact.	All students shall acquire sufficient knowledge of the techniques of learning to enable them to become lifelong learners.

DEPARTMENTAL PURPOSES
    Departments involved: English
                            Social Studies
                            Art
                            Music
                            Foreign Languages

FOREIGN LANGUAGE DEPARTMENT PURPOSES

Each learner enrolled in foreign languages shall acquire:

a. an understanding and appreciation of persons belonging to social, cultural and ethnic groups different from his own;

b. an ability to communicate orally, in writing, and nonverbally with speakers of another language;

c. a knowledge of how to learn a foreign language and attitudes conducive to such learning.

COURSE PURPOSES

Level I Spanish

1. The student will become aware of the differences in family customs in Mexico and the United States.

2. The students will indicate the basic differences in customs between the upper class and the lower class in Mexico with special emphasis on eating habits and food, dating, marriage, and educational opportunities.

3. The students will recognize certain famous Mexican singers and some of the more popular Mexican songs.

TERMINAL COURSE OBJECTIVES

Level I Spanish

1. The student will view a short film about a Mexican family at dinner in *La Familia Fernandez;* he will then indicate on the test sheet given him which of ten behaviors listed are similar to those found in a typical American family and which are different.

2. The student will be given twenty statements of customs such as:

(a) A sixteen-year-old frequently runs errands for his mother in the family car.

(b) A seventeen-year-old girl usually does not go out on a date unchaperoned.

(c) Teenagers who baby-sit for families other than their own are usually paid by the hour.

The student will indicate by checking whether the custom is typical of Mexico or of the United States; he will further indicate whether it is a custom that is generally found in the upper, middle, or lower classes, or in all social classes.

If the statement applies to neither culture he will leave all spaces blank.

3. When a tape of five popular Mexican songs (performed by three different popular singers) is played, the student will indicate the following on his answer sheet:

(a) the name of the song (to be selected from a list of 20 provided on the answer sheet);

(b) the name of the singer (to be selected from a list of 10 provided on the answer sheet).

All songs and singers are listed on the sheet attached; recordings of these songs are available in the language laboratory.

The departmental purposes given above lend direction to the entire foreign language program. They tell to some degree what should occur at *each level* of language learning since they speak of *each learner.* They do not put off any of the parts of the goal until the final sequence. This goal is not to be confused with course purposes, since the latter assign specific responsibility to a given level or course; that is why they are called *course* purposes.

Let us examine the process that would be used in goal refinement to break the departmental purpose down into course purposes at the various levels. We will assume that the language being studied is Spanish. The first step would be to assign content to the various levels. Consider goal I:

LEVEL I
Mexico
Family Customs
Famous Singers
Classes in the Society

LEVEL II
Cuba, Puerto Rico
Leisure Time Activities
Famous Artists
Problems of Spanish-Speaking Peoples
  Living in the United States

LEVEL III
South America
History and Origins
Famous Monuments
Revolutions—How They Are Born and Bred

LEVEL IV
Spain
Current Philosophies
Great Men of Letters
Implications of Words Such as *Hermano*

A similar division and assignment may be made of the various affective skills: Developing awareness, responsiveness, understanding, accepting, valuing.

Once the skills have been assigned and the content has been assigned by levels, the team begins to write the purposes for each level. Teachers must bear in mind the caution that affective objectives can overlap with cognitive objectives. (Krathwohl, *et al.,* 1964, p. 54).

Some measure of individuality is also to be encouraged. One school may choose to concentrate on Mexico for two years but to vary the points in content and the skills; another may choose to vary both the content and the skills as well as the geographic area being covered. These decisions reflect the thinking of those who are trying to refine the district or school philosophy into course purposes. Then the team must phrase the purposes so that they provide specific direction or guidance for the terminal course objectives. If the purposes are well constructed, the objectives will be much simpler to write.

Before constructing the course purposes, the team should review input from all available sources about the community, the students, their needs, and their aspirations; this broad base of input should include the thinking of teachers from other departments, of administrators, of counselors, and also of parents and students.

Please notice in the course and departmental purposes that, although the verbs "become aware," "understand," and "recognize" are not "behavioral verbs (since they do not indicate how the student will demonstrate what he has done), they serve to refine the philosophical statement and goals into a specific philosophical direction for one level of language learning. The task of the team is one of refinement and review.

Before any other steps are taken, the purposes should be reviewed and revised by those who will be teaching the course. If the purposes do not reflect their thinking, they cannot be used effectively as a basis for teaching. This does not imply that every person must be in one hundred percent agreement with every purpose; as in all good ventures there must be compromise. But the totality of the purposes should bear the endorsement of those who will be teaching the course. Otherwise the purposes will become "paper purposes," stuffed into the first available desk drawer. The purposes should also be reviewed by any supervisors and administrators who have responsibility for the program since it is folly to write a set of performance objectives only to find that the objectives are not consonant with the thinking of the administration. This is the part of the process that takes time, but it usually bears very good fruit. Often this is the moment when disagreements surface, when departments become aware of what many have suspected for years: there is a basic difference of opinion as to what should be accomplished in any course. If time is spent ironing out these differences at *this* level, the work of the next level will be immensely simplified.

There are several considerations which should enter into the acceptance or rejection of a purpose. For example:

Is the purpose related to the goal or philosophy?

Is the purpose realistic?

Is the purpose specific enough? (see Jenks, *et al.,* 1972, Unit II, pp. 29-30).

Once the purposes have been reviewed and accepted, the next task consists of refining the course purposes into measurable performance objectives. We begin with terminal course objectives: What do we expect students to be able to do at the end of the level or course that will demonstrate the competencies and proficiencies that we wish them to attain?

Various criteria may be used in reviewing sets of terminal course objectives. In recent materials prepared by Jenks and his colleagues at the Far West Laboratory, attention is called to three basic criteria for terminal course objectives: guidance, relevance, and feasibility. These three criteria are defined and refined as follows:

GUIDANCE: Terminal course objectives must provide directions to the prospective users. They must be stated clearly so that the intent is plainly and uniformly understood by the users. As the specificity increases through the refinement process, greater clarity should appear. The following questions might be asked to determine whether or not a specific terminal course objective meets the guidance criterion:

Does the objective clearly indicate the desired student behavior?

Is the verb used (e.g., "identify," "solve," "compare") specific enough that misinterpretation will be minimized?

Does the objective indicate the curricular area in which the behavior is to occur?

Can responsibility and accountability for the objective be assigned to one or more curricular subject areas?

Can you measure the attainment of this objective?

RELEVANCE: A terminal course objective is relevant if it is meaningful to the learner, if it is related to the educational goal from which it is derived, and if it is desirable in terms of the present and future expectations of the school and its related groups. The following questions might be raised to determine whether or not a specific terminal course objective meets the criterion of relevance:

Does the objective satisfy the present and future needs of the learner?

Does the objective specify a behavior that will have immediate and long-range use to the learner?

Will the attainment of the objective help the student to become an effective person in his society?

Will the attainment of the objective have any ill effects on the learner?

Will the achievement of the objective lead to the attainment of the long-range goal from which it is derived?

Does the objective reflect what students, parents, citizens, and educators consider to be a desirable educational aspiration?

Would students consider the objective important to them?

Would parents and citizens react positively toward student achievement of the objective?

Do educational specialists and subject matter specialists generally agree that this is a worthwhile objective?

Do teachers and other members of the school staff consider this a desirable objective?

FEASIBILITY: A terminal course objective is considered feasible if there is a good probability of its being achieved. Decisions on the number and the scope of objectives must be based on past experience. One must also raise the question of the feasibility of a set of terminal course objectives. Although each objective in and of itself might be feasible, the collection of objectives might prove unrealistic within the time span allotted. Questions that might be used to determine the feasibility of terminal course objectives are:

Does the objective have a good probability of being achieved?

Is it consistent with student and staff abilities?

Is enough known about the type of learning implied to ensure a chance of its accomplishment?

Has successful attainment of this or similar objectives occurred in other schools?

Have attempts to achieve this or similar objectives failed in other schools? If yes, why?

Is the achievement of this objective practical in view of organizational capacities, limits, and constraints?

Is the benefit of achieving the objective worth the costs in money, personnel, planning, and time?

If the objective deviates from present practices, is it desirable in light of its foreseeable social impact? Is it desirable in light of the possible consequences for the institution?

Does the objective conflict with the values and beliefs of the community, of students, staff, or special interest groups? If so, is it desirable in view of the strategies that may have to be implemented to meet and refute criticism? (Jenks, *et al.*, 1972, Unit II).

If all the objectives meet the criteria of guidance, relevance, and feasibility then we move to a review of the entire set of objectives; we screen out those that do not belong and add those which are lacking.

In reviewing the set of terminal course objectives we should ask the following questions:

1. Does the set contain an appropriate representation of cognitive behaviors?

2. Does the set contain an adequate representation of affective behaviors? (Cognitive and affective behaviors are discussed in depth in Chapter VI of this book.)

3. Is the set of objectives broad enough to cover the subject adequately?

4. Are all of the objectives internally consistent?

For this process we should begin by aligning each terminal course objective with a purpose. There should be at least one terminal course objective for each purpose. There should be no terminal course objective that is not connected to a purpose. If there are some terminal course objectives unconnected to a purpose they should either be jettisoned or a new purpose should be written and added to those already accepted. It goes without saying that the new purpose must be a refinement of the department purposes, the goal, and the philosophy. There are many objectives that we have traditionally asked students to meet because we met them in our day or because the text includes material about them. If we include objectives that do not carry out our purposes, we may find it no longer feasible to include all the objectives that do complement them. We have reached a point of decision making. Remember: It is much easier to add new objectives than it is to delete those which are not feasible, and sets of objectives that lack feasibility are worth little either to students or teachers.

After we have reviewed the set of objectives, we then turn to refining the terminal course objectives into learning objectives, to implementing the learning objectives with resources and activities, and to preparing lessons plans and schedules.

SUMMARY OF THE THREE APPROACHES TO WRITING PERFORMANCE OBJECTIVES

FEATURE	CONVERSION SYSTEM	ADAPTIVE SYSTEM	GOAL REFINEMENT SYSTEM
Point of Departure	One text or set of materials.	Eclectically chosen curriculum materials (i.e., one text supplemented by other materials; multiple texts, etc.).	The refinement of the school or district educational philosophy whereby the selection of curriculum materials occurs only after performance objectives have been written
Principal Activity	The teacher determines what the learner is expected to do at the end of each lesson. (This information can often be gleaned by examining the accompanying publisher's tests.)	The teacher writes purposes and course and learning objectives which can be achieved with the eclectically chosen materials at hand.	The teacher or team of teachers creates a curriculum "from scratch" by breaking down the school philosophy into school purposes, departmental purposes, terminal course objectives, and learning objectives; and by seeking the necessary resources and activities to achieve all of these.
Advantages	a) Simplicity: Purposes have already been established and content already sequenced by textbook author.	a) Teachers start out where they are and with whatever materials they have at hand and wish to use.	a) The entire curriculum can be organized and sequenced to meet the needs of individual learners.

FEATURE	CONVERSION SYSTEM	ADAPTIVE SYSTEM	GOAL REFINEMENT SYSTEM
	b) Less time, money, or effort needs to be expended than with either of the other two approaches. c) The work can easily be divided up among several teachers.	b) Teachers (not textbook author) select the resources and activities students need.	b) The curriculum is based upon input from students, teachers, administrators, parents, and the community. c) A change in textbooks does not necessarily result in an obsolete curriculum.
Disadvantages	a) The curriculum is determined by the textbook. A change in text requires redoing much of the work; hence encourages retention of obsolete texts. b) Articulation with programs using other textbooks is not facilitated. c) If teachers do not subscribe to the philosophy of the textbook author, they will be unhappy with this system.	a) The temptation exists to undertake too much curriculum reform, hence never to get the objectives written. b) It is difficult to add content to, or omit content from, the materials one is teaching. c) It is only a halfway measure and as such may fail to satisfy teachers or students who desire major curricular reform.	a) It involves the greatest expenditures of time, money, and effort. b) The opportunity for the work to "bog down" in disagreement is always present.

IV. PLANNING and
DESIGNING A CURRICULUM

Those who are quickest to innovate, who are most creative in implementing new ideas, who have the nerve to venture forth, often lack the organizational skills that make innovation effective. They often fail to consider in advance the problems they will encounter and possible solutions to these problems. They frequently also fail to consider various approaches to the innovation, hence fail to make prior decisions which could help to ensure success. There is no single format for all situations. Some schools and teachers spend so much time planning an innovation that the innovation is passé before it is ever implemented; others jump in blindly with the hope that they will be able to solve any and all problems they may encounter. The following steps are offered to stimulate your thinking so that you will develop the best procedures for implementing change in your program:

1. *Assess the current situation in your department and in your school.* If all is running smoothly, if your enrollment is increasing, if your students are happy, if the parents, legislature, and trustees are supporting your efforts financially and enthusiastically, then perhaps your reasons for innovating are less pressing. Nevertheless, you may feel that the status quo will not be so attractive in a few years; you may sense certain trends which

could alter your comfortable situation. This must be a part of your assessment. If you are *presently* having problems however, you will find an audience that will be more receptive to change. If you begin by involving others in the assessment of needs and in the decision to change, you will provide your innovation with a greater chance for success. List your needs in order of priority. Do performance objectives offer some solutions to problems that you are currently facing? Do they help clarify the present curriculum? Do they provide a basis for change?

2. Decide *with your colleagues* upon an approach to the writing of objectives if your needs assessment above has indicated that the writing of objectives may be a solution to one or more of your problems. Consider the possible approaches to performance objective writing detailed in the preceding chapter of this book. Then formulate a plan with your colleagues and agree upon a tentative calendar. Schedule your first three meetings and assign each person a specific task. Do not worry if the plan chosen is not in your opinion the best one. A plan that has group approval has more chance of ultimate success, and there will be time to refine it later. Decide upon the in-service training that is needed. Read all the available literature you can, formulate questions, bring in outside speakers, and study any sets of objectives that are at your disposal.

3. When your group has formulated a plan *discuss* it with your department chairman, supervisor, principal, or dean. He may be able to offer some good suggestions, and he may also be able to help you secure funds or consultants for in-service training. Involve your superiors early and keep them informed.

4. Schedule few unstructured meetings. Ask people to prepare purposes or objectives and let the general discussion emerge from these. Teachers love to talk, but a discussion based on specifics is usually more pertinent and rewarding.

5. Involve students at the discussion level especially in constructing course purposes. You may want to invite some parents to your first committee session; urge them to share with you their feelings as to what students should be able to do after one, two, or three years study in your subject area. They will have a more positive attitude to the innovation for having been involved, even if you do not heed all their advice.

6. If your approach includes the writing of course purposes, be sure to get agreement on the purposes before continuing.

7. Experiment with some of your objectives as you begin to write them. Try one limited set on a class and evaluate that set after you finish the unit. Did the students feel that they learned more or less? Can they tell you how to strengthen your objectives? We often forget the "customer" in

the educational enterprise, and indeed students can be very valuable associates.

8. Don't try to solve all your problems at once. Put in writing any problem which comes up and consider several of these at each meeting.

9. If possible, visit some other schools where your proposed innovation is implemented and determine to what extent teachers are using objectives. Do you think the use of performance objectives would improve their students' learning?

10. Don't spend a lot of money mimeographing and binding your first set of objectives; you probably will want to change the contents several times. Prepare the objectives as inexpensively as possible.

11. Examine any relevant objectives that are already on the market. You may find some that will work "as is" with your students or you may find some that can be adapted to your students. It is most unlikely that you will come upon a set that completely matches the needs of your students.

12. Write objectives for only one level of learning at one time. Some states have mandated policies that require courses to be stated in performance terms by a certain date. However, it is much easier to put all your energy into one course before turning to another.

13. Remember that "Rome was not built in a day." Your planning may indicate that you cannot accomplish everything in one academic or calendar year. It is better to set up your program in two or three phases than to kill yourself and your colleagues by attempting too much too soon.

Once your plans have been delineated, schedule regular meetings and provide people with deadlines. Remember that teachers are busy. They, too, will tend to procrastinate unless they have specific assignments. Encourage your teachers to be honest with each other but not overly critical. A spelling error or absence of an accent mark is not a true indication of a person's competence or lack of it. By working together the team can lighten the load for each member.

V. SELECTING OBJECTIVES

Your plans are made. You have decided on an approach to your performance curriculum, and you have prepared a set of course purposes. The time has now come to begin the task of writing the objectives. While dealing with purposes you spoke in lofty or general terms, but now you must deal with specifics. Where and how do you begin?

In most instances it is preferable to construct terminal course objectives first. How does a group of teachers at a first meeting set about determining terminal course objectives? There are many possibilities.

Ideally, if a group has elected the goal refinement system, teachers would begin by discussing philosophically and pedagogically the best way to implement the course purposes. One would consider questions such as the following:

1. What skills should the student possess at the end of level I? level II? level III? level IV?
2. How should the student be able to demonstrate these skills?
3. What vocabulary and structure should form part of the student's productive skills? (conversation and writing)
4. What vocabulary and structure should form part of the student's receptive skills? (listening and reading)

5. What knowledge of culture, civilization, history, art, literature should the student control?

6. How should the student demonstrate control of the items mentioned in 3-5 above?

7. What level of mastery can we reasonably expect of the student?

8. What are reasonable expectations for skill control, content mastery, etc., within the established time limits?

9. What attitudes and feelings do we want students to develop? How will we want them to demonstrate these attitudes and feelings?

Some teachers may find these questions difficult to cope with. They may find it easier to *begin with known specifics* and then deal with such questions as the above at a later date. *It is important to remember that a feeling of accomplishment and success is essential to a team.* Teachers may also be somewhat reassured to discover that they have already been using performance objectives, even though they may not have called them that. How can one help teachers to discover those objectives they may already have established?

Begin by looking at last year's final examination. This will provide a point of departure. If it was a departmental exam, some commonalities have been established. Look at the various sections of the examination. Was there a reading passage? a listening comprehension section? a verb section? a vocabulary section? a free composition or a guided composition? Was there a section where students were asked to rewrite sentences from one tense to another or from one person to another? Was there a speaking section where the student had to speak or answer questions directly, either "live" or on tape? Was there a grammar section? a section of culture? a pronunciation section? a spelling section or a *dictée*?

List the sections horizontally on the blackboard. If there was no departmental test, then ask each teacher to list the sections of his test. The board would then look like this:

Jones	Listening Comp.	Reading	Dictée	Rewrite	Vocab.	
Smith		Reading	Pronun.	Grammar	Vocab.	Verbs
Brown	Listening Comp.		Dictée	Grammar	Vocab.	Verbs

It is plain to see that there are some areas in common and some peculiar to one or more individual tests. *Begin with the common areas* and ask the next question. *What skill or skills did the teachers ask their students to demonstrate in each of these areas?* Under each section list the skills the student demonstrated on the individual examination. Your list might now look like this:

Listening Comprehension	Verbs	Vocabulary
Selected written multiple-choice answer to a question read by the teacher.	Wrote the correct form for the infinitive in parentheses; was told which tense to use.	Wrote isolated words in the target language when given the English.

If the test was not a departmental test it is probable that various teachers asked students to demonstrate knowledge in different ways. If so, list all the means of demonstrating competency. The list could look like this:

Reading

Jones   Student read passage and selected appropriate multiple choice answers in the target language to questions asked in target language.

Brown   Student read passage and wrote a summary in English.

Smith   Student read passage and wrote answers (in the target language) to questions asked in target language.

Morris   Student read passage and wrote in English answers to questions asked in the target language.

Stevens   Students read passages and translated underlined key sections.

Obviously there is a wide range here, but it is not impossible to find this amount of difference in a large department. *It is important not to let teachers get bogged down by arguing which "method" is preferable at this point.* There will be time for that later. The task is simply to assemble and codify information with which you can work.

Next, *under each section try to list the content covered.* Did the exam test all the material covered that year? the last two chapters?

Was there variance from one section to the next? Was the student informed of the content coverage of the exam or was he told to "learn everything"? List first what the exam covered and then put a star by those sections where the student knew the content coverage at least two days in advance of the examination.

The next part is the most difficult. *Ask the teachers to list the passing grade for the total examination. Then ask them to reconstruct as best they can what percentage of each section the average student achieved.* If they do not remember, they can look up any records they may have of the examination scores prior to the next meeting. It is a *range* of achievement that you are seeking, for you will have a difficult time persuading teachers to be realistic in writing objectives unless they perceive that they have settled for reasonable scores in the past. All teachers like to think that they have high standards, and many of us forget those dull dark moments we spent grading last June's examinations when we wondered whether certain of our students had learned anything. Such memories should encourage us to set realistic standards.

Next, add to this list any other type of evaluation that was a part of the *final grade.* Do not include quizzes given during the last marking period, but do include special projects such as an oral report, a written report, a performance of a skit or scene from a play, i.e., anything that would measure additional competencies that might have been evaluated at a time other than that of the final examination. Add these to your list, delineate the skills demonstrated, and list the content covered. Then try to determine the criteria for a passing grade.

When you have completed this task, you will have sketched the type of performance objectives you have been, perhaps unconsciously, assigning to students. These objectives may in no way represent what you feel students ought to be doing, *but they do represent what they have been doing.* Now, as an exercise, you must defend your expectations. There is no gain if teachers write an entirely new set of performance objectives but continue to adhere to what they expected previously; so the next step is to ask each teacher to specify as positively as possible why he included the various sections he placed on his final examination.

Teachers usually have some reason for what they include in an examination. It is absolutely necessary at this point that they listen to one another. They may find that they have much in common but have simply used different testing procedures. They may find that they hold widely divergent ideas on language teaching. If the former is true, the task is relatively easy. You simply proceed to a discussion of the most effective way of demonstrating a skill. Then you discuss how much content you can reasonably expect your students to master in each of the areas. Next you develop the level of mastery that you expect in each area. *Remember,* the greater the amount of content, the less proficiency or level of mastery you can demand if you keep within a single time limit. If your demands are unrealistic, students will be unable to meet them.

If your group holds widely divergent ideas on language learning and language teaching, you will need to utilize your purposes as a springboard against which you can measure these divergent points of view. Which are compatible with the course purposes? Which are not? Perhaps this is a good time to consult students, parents, counselors, administrators, as well as the teachers themselves, so the department need not be divided against itself. Do not let the discussion get out of hand. One way to settle differences is a rating or voting system. Take all the areas listed in each person's test and put them on the board. If you have eight items you will have eight points. Then ask each person to rate the eight items in order of importance. They can distribute their eight points any way they wish:

Jones
1. Listening Comprehension
2. Dictée
3. Pronunciation
4. Vocabulary
5. Rewrite
6. Reading
7. Verbs
8. Grammar

Smith
1. Grammar
2. Verbs
3. Vocabulary
4. Reading
5. Dictée

6. Pronunciation
7. Rewrite
8. Listening Comprehension

Brown
1. Listening Comprehension
2. Dictée
3. Vocabulary
4. Pronunciation
5. Rewrite
6. Reading
7. Verbs
8. Grammar

Morris
1. Listening Comprehension
2. Reading
3. Rewrite
4. Vocabulary
5. Dictée
6. Pronunciation
7. Grammar
8. Verbs

When all have finished, put the point count of each individual by the item, and you will quickly see which items the group as a whole considers important:

Composite Points

1. Listening Comp.	1		3. Vocabulary	4	
	8			3	
	1			3	
	1	1		4	2-3
	11			14	

2. Dictée	2		4. Reading	6	
	5	2-3		4	
	2			6	
	5			2	4
	14			18	

5. Pronunciation	3		7. Grammar	8	
	6			1	
	4			8	7
	6	5		7	
	19			24	

6. Rewrite	5		8. Verbs	7	
	7			7	
	5			7	
	3	6		8	8
	20			29	

The composite ranking would then look like this:

1.	Listening Comprehension	11 pts.
2-3.	Dictée	14 pts.
2-3.	Vocabulary	14 pts.
4.	Reading	18 pts.
5.	Pronunciation	19 pts.
6.	Rewrite	20 pts.
7.	Grammar	24 pts.
8.	Verbs	29 pts.

The composite answer may please nobody. This is the time to begin to reassess priorities. In most schools there will be common agreement on the majority of the material and a difference of opinion on a lesser percentage of the matters considered. Once again, *begin in the areas of agreement.*

If you have chosen the conversion system, you may have problems of agreement. Ask each teacher to read the teacher's manual, tests, and any other material prepared by the publisher to ascertain what terminal course objectives the textbook authors and publishers have in mind. If these teachers have used the book previously they may be able to list the terminal course objectives determined by the textbook authors.

It is possible that with the conversion system you may wish to begin with learning objectives instead of with terminal course objectives. You may feel that the terminal course objectives will emerge from the learning objectives. Nevertheless, even here, it would be preferable and advisable to determine what skills and competencies students would be expected to possess at the end of the course.

If you have chosen the adaptive system, you will at this point want to ask each teacher to prepare terminal course objectives for one skill area, such as listening comprehension. At the next meeting you may want to invite the teachers of the next level to attend and to share opinions with you on what the terminal course objectives of the previous level should be. Remind each teacher to check that his or her terminal course objectives reflect the purposes.

Whatever system you have selected, impress upon your teachers that they should list what *the student is to do* in a testing situation to demonstrate what he has learned. The student is going to *recite* a dialogue, *answer* questions orally, *ask* questions orally, *summarize* orally, *read* aloud, *select* answers, *write* answers in English or in the target language, *translate, rewrite* sentences, *fill in* the blanks, *write* a composition, *analyze* a work of literature in writing, etc. Caution teachers to avoid verbs such as "learn," "know," "understand," and "appreciate," for such verbs do not tell a student what he really is expected to do.

Before the end of the first work session, have each teacher write at least one performance objective in the area where he or she will be working alone. Choose the wording that most appeals to your group and adopt it as a format. You may address the performance objective to the student:

Under what conditions?	You will hear on tape a short telephone conversation
Time limit?	(2 minutes) between a boy and a girl about the weather,
Content specification?	their date that night and their friends. You will then hear 10 oral questions based on the tape. You will also hear three possible answers read.
Other limitations?	The tape will not be repeated.
What will the student do?	Circle 1, 2, or 3 on your answer sheet.
To what level of mastery?	To receive a *B* you must have at least 8 out of 10 correct answers.

Ask each teacher to prepare a set of objectives for the next meeting. Allow a suitable time interval before the next meeting, but do not let too much time pass before calling the group together. Enthusiasm will grow as the project progresses and as you have something to show for your efforts.

Ask each teacher to bring to the next meeting enough copies of his or her objectives so that all have a set with which to work. Read through several sets of objectives before beginning to critique them. Then take one area at a time; you might begin by asking:

1. Does the objective state what the student is to do?
2. Is the means of demonstrating knowledge appropriate to the objective?
3. Is the content coverage realistic?
4. Are the conditions and time limits realistic and appropriate?
5. Is the objective relevant to the learner's needs, interests, and abilities?
6. Does the objective implement one or more of the course purposes?

After the terminal course objectives have been agreed upon, the teachers will next break down these terminal course objectives into learning objectives. A single learning objective may take a few minutes, a class period, a week, or several weeks. *All learning objectives must lead to a terminal course objective.* If the student perceives this he will see reason and value in seemingly irrelevant tasks. Many of our drills are used to accomplish learning objectives, but students have not recognized this fact and have viewed the drills as a waste of time. It is true, for example, that in traveling in France I have seldom had a conversation like the following:

It is raining. Yes, and it was raining yesterday.
I eat spinach regularly. I used to eat spinach regularly.

Most such drills are somewhat comic in nature, but they can and do play a vital role in language learning in that they are steps to a bigger objective. Consider the following terminal course objective:

The student will use the appropriate forms of the *passé composé* and the *imparfait* in recounting events that occurred a week ago.
(Content specified on attached page.)

Obviously this objective has several developmental steps:

a. the student must recognize the forms of the *imparfait* and *passé composé;*

b. the student must be able to reconstruct the forms of the *imparfait* and *passé composé;*

c. the student must control sufficient vocabulary including verb meanings;

d. the student must determine which of these two tenses is indicated on which occasion;

e. the student must be able to combine steps *a-d.*

Each of these steps could represent a learning objective, and mastery of each could be asked before the student is allowed to proceed to the next step. However, the student knows that the terminal course objective is the really important matter, and if he can bypass the intermediate steps, he should be encouraged to do so.

From this point, each teacher is free to determine those activities which in his opinion will best help the student to reach the learning objectives. Teachers can and should use a variety of different activities to reach a learning objective. Take the following objective as an example:

> When given a 10-line paragraph of French prose the student will demonstrate recognition of the forms of the *imparfait* and *passé composé* by underlining all *passé composé* forms once and all *imparfait* forms twice within a five-minute period.
> Criterion: 90%

In order to help the student reach this objective the teacher can:

> a. present the forms of the two tenses on the board;
> b. assign a lesson in the text that explains the differences;
> c. ask the student to memorize the *passé composé* and *imparfait* of two model verbs;
> d. give the student a dittoed handout that explains the two tenses;
> e. ask the student to memorize a short dialogue containing forms of the two tenses;
> f. ask the student to identify the forms of the two tenses within drills;
> g. ask the student to complete French sentences by selecting the correct form of the verb;
> h. ask the student to underline the *passé composé* once and the *imparfait* forms twice within sentences or a paragraph;
> i. assign a quick-change oral drill for each of the two tenses;
> j. ask students to read aloud in French a short paragraph and identify the *imparfait* and *passé composé* forms;
> k. ask the student to answer in French questions that contain the forms of the two tenses; etc.

To make *all* students do *all* of the activities listed above would probably be inefficient and damaging to student morale. That is, if students can do the majority of the activities easily, they should certainly be able to meet the objective. Some of these activities may in fact be leading to the next objective, but teachers are faced with the judicious choice of activities that will first of all help the student to meet the assigned objective. The selection of the activity is determined by the age, maturity, ability, interests, and needs of the learner. If our activities are chosen to meet carefully specified, well-considered objectives, and if these objectives implement purposes that are agreed upon by teachers, parents, administrators, and students, then our classes will indeed be relevant.

We might well, at this point, consider some safeguards that can keep our activities and our objectives from becoming repetitious and boring. One such safeguard is a taxonomy, and this is the topic of the next chapter.

VI. TAXONOMIES and CLASSIFICATIONS

In education, a taxonomy is a system of classification which divides learning into several levels beginning with the simplest or lowest level and continuing to the most complex or highest level. The purpose of taxonomies, according to Benjamin Bloom (1956, p. 1), one of the pathfinders in this area, is to provide a classification of the goals of an educational system. Looking at learning taxonomically should help one see the emphasis given to certain behaviors by a particular set of educational goals, plans, or objectives.

Before considering the role and importance of taxonomies in the writing of performance objectives, however, one needs to pose the following question: Is the prime purpose of stating the curriculum in performance terms to ascertain what teachers are currently demanding of students? That is to say, is the first concern one of clarifying to teachers, students, parents, and administrators what is actually taking place? If so, taxonomies need not be considered during the writing process. If teachers learning to write performance objectives begin to worry about the classification of these objectives, they may become discouraged and abandon the project completely. Therefore, especially with the conversion system, the teacher's first effort should concentrate on creating the performance objectives themselves.

This process should, however, be followed by an evaluation and a screening of the objectives. A taxonomy can now serve effectively as a guide in the evaluation process. Revision centers around the deletion of those objectives deemed inappropriate and the addition of those that are needed but lacking.

Bloom and his colleagues have delineated three areas or "domains" of learning: the cognitive, the psychomotor, and the affective. According to Bloom *et al.*, the cognitive domain is the area of learning which deals with facts and knowledge, the psychomotor domain is that area which deals with activities that are primarily physical, and the affective domain is the area of attitudes and feelings. That is, a cognitive objective deals with what a learner should *know*, a psychomotor objective deals with what a learner should physically *do,* and an affective objective deals with how a learner should *feel.* In his first volume Bloom listed the following stages of cognitive learning: knowledge, comprehension, application, analysis, synthesis, and evaluation.

In a companion volume (Krathwohl, *et al.,* 1964, p. 35), Bloom and his co-authors list the following stages of affective behaviors: receiving, responding, valuing, organization, and characterization by a value or value complex.

Rebecca Valette made a preliminary adaptation of the Bloom taxonomy to foreign language instruction in *Directions in Foreign Language Testing* (1969). Valette and Renée Disick have produced the most recent (1972) taxonomy for foreign language learning *(Modern Language Performance Objectives and Individualization: A Handbook).* Unlike Bloom these two authors combine the cognitive and psychomotor areas. They list five stages of subject matter learning: mechanical skills (the lowest), knowledge, transfer, communication, and criticism (the highest). For affective goals they give receptivity (lowest), responsiveness, appreciation, internalization, and characterization (the highest). They then provide examples of both an internal behavior and an external behavior for each stage. Part II of their book is devoted to classifying student behaviors in the field of foreign languages under each of these stages and giving examples of the same.

The question might be raised: "What is the need for taxonomies in writing performance objectives?" As I have suggested above, taxonomies are primarily useful in studying an entire curriculum, in reviewing a set of performance objectives; they usually do not have a role to play in writing the objectives. If a team is using the goal refinement system, however, it may prefer to consider a taxonomy at the time of writing the objectives, since the goal refinement process is a lengthy one. By the time the team has reached the stage of writing objectives, it has already become accustomed to the process of refining goal statements. That is why the use of a classification system might not seem so formidable in this particular approach.

Nevertheless, it is easier to understand and review performance objectives than it is to construct them. If at any point a team becomes confused, it should first master the art of constructing objectives. Then it should move to the matter of reviewing, assessing, revising, deleting, and adding.

The devision as to whether or not to use taxonomies in the initial writing of performance objectives must remain one for the individual teacher or team of teachers to make. It is certainly true that at some stage in the process a taxonomy will be very useful. It will quickly indicate, for example, whether or not a specific curriculum is composed only of simple, low-level cognitive objectives. It can also indicate that the curriculum is tedious since the same type of learning may be demanded of students in the fourth and fifth years as 'in the first and second. The contention of this writer is that the process of writing performance objectives must be simplified so that teachers, busy as they are, may have reasonable hopes of completing the task and using the objectives in the classroom. A judicious mixture of various types of cognitive objectives, psychomotor objectives, and affective objectives should be selected.

The review, assessment, and screening may indicate that there is a gap between the objectives and the purposes. If this occurs it is possible that the team has chosen the wrong type of objective to implement a purpose. If the teacher wishes the student to appreciate concepts and trends but asks him only to demonstrate mastery of dates, identifications, and definitions, then he has created an obvious curricular gap. By consulting a taxonomy the team can determine the different type of objective necessary to implement the stated purpose.

Foreign language educators should especially consider taxonomies in the construction of a four-year curriculum. Too often only the content is varied, and students are asked to engage in the same types of activities and to work toward the same objectives year after year. They fill in blanks the first year, they fill in blanks the second year, and again throughout the third and fourth years. They answer simple questions on different books from level I through level IV. If they fail to develop conversational skills, their failure may reflect the fact that their teachers have confronted them with but few spoken-language objectives demanding analysis, synthesis, and evaluation. It is indeed valuable to consider the taxonomy a guidebook as we *select* objectives. When we examine our courses once they have been cast in performance terms, we can delete within those areas where there is an overabundance of objectives of one type, and we can add objectives in areas where they are deficient.

The Valette and Disick book treats the subject of taxonomies in depth. There is no need to repeat that treatment here, and the reader is encouraged to consult both that work and the two volumes written by Bloom and Krathwohl and their associates for a more thorough study of this subject.

VII. CRITERION-REFERENCED TESTING and GRADING PROCEDURES

Valette and Disick have defined criterion-referenced tests as "all tests used to measure whether or not performance objectives have been attained" (Valette and Disick, 1972, p. 67). Such tests should, of course, play a major role in any curriculum based on performance objectives. After all, if the main purpose of performance objectives is to clarify for both teacher and student what is expected of the student, then it is imperative that the test be based solely on these expectations. It is most unfair for a teacher to indicate the most important things to be learned in a course and then to test and grade the student on different items, which is what has sometimes happened in the past. Teachers have been known to emphasize strongly the salient points in a lesson and then include on the test small bits of information that the student may have overlooked in his attention to the main points. It is perfectly fair to expect a student to have mastered either content or skills to a high level of accuracy *provided that* the student knows exactly what is expected of him. *A criterion-referenced test is one which relates each test item directly to the objectives of the lesson.* The test is based exclusively on content which has been specified to the student before he begins the lesson. Thus he knows exactly what he must learn and how he must be able to demonstrate it.

Achievement testing, according to Robert Glaser (in Popham, 1971, pp. 6-7), provides two different kinds of information: 1) the degree to which the student has attained criterion performance, on the one hand; and 2) the relative ordering of individuals with respect to their test performance. Criterion-referenced tests yield the first kind of information; norm-referenced tests yield the second kind.

The use of criterion-referenced tests should also reveal exactly what an entering student has already learned and what he still needs to master. College professors, for example, could determine with such tests which students are proficient in one area but deficient in another.

Criterion-referenced tests are built on specified content and skills. Consider the following performance objective:

> The student will rewrite twenty sentences from the present to the preterite.
> The verbs chosen will be from Chapters 4 through 8.

The student who is faced with this objective knows that he must manipulate in writing twenty verb forms from those verbs in Chapters 4 through 8. He is responsible for all those verbs, but he need not worry about verbs in other chapters. If this is the first time the student has encountered the preterite, this objective would cover sufficient content. On the other hand, if this were an advanced course, one might wish to use a different content specification. If the objective is important primarily for the skill involved, the content should be limited. On the other hand, if the student already has control of the skill, then content can be the main focus.

The second part of the objective should tell the student what constitutes an acceptable performance. We are now dealing in value terms. If the teacher uses an A to F grading system, he should specify what is expected for an A, B, C, etc.; many teachers do not like to indicate the cut-off for passing, but that is precisely what students want to know. Where content has been specified in advance, teachers can demand a higher level of mastery with a clear conscience. The student is no longer spending time playing games; he knows what he is expected to do.

Criterion-referenced tests differ from other types of tests in that their purpose is to measure only whether or not a student knows a specific skill, a specific bit of content or a combination of the two. They are *not* used to measure how well a student does in relation to others in the class, but rather how well a student does compared with an absolute standard. They do *not* measure a student's total knowledge of the subject on a random basis. It is this writer's contention that there is a place in the curriculum for *all* types of achievement testing: criterion-referenced tests, norm-referenced standardized tests such as those given by the College Entrance Examination Board, and random sampling tests such as those made by textbook authors, by language departments, and by colleges for use as placement tests. The difficulty arises when these different types of tests are misused in the learning process.

When the student learns specific information as he does in the first two years of language learning, criterion-referenced tests should be the order of the day. The student should know specifically what is important, to what degree it is important to the teacher (hence to himself), and how much time he needs to devote to the subject to reach the level of mastery. Teachers must choose: do they prefer students to have a random sampling and partial control over a great amount of content, or do they prefer students to have a high level of mastery over a smaller amount of content, or do they prefer a mixture of the two? Notice that *mixture* is the key word. Most teachers claim that they expect a high level of mastery over a large amount of material, and this is exactly what frustrates substantial numbers of students who do not care to devote countless hours to the subject, but who also have no desire to receive mediocre or poor grades. If the teacher can direct the student to the important elements in the course, then the average student should be able to achieve acceptable results without spending an undue amount of time. The student must then be evaluated on what he has been told is important and must be held accountable for it. Criterion-referenced tests are the only fair means of assessing the student's progress in this setting.

One might ask, "Of what value are norm-referenced tests? When should they be given?" Norm-referenced tests can show teachers or departments how well their curriculum and their students stack up against others. They are best administered toward the end of the year, and, in this writer's opinion, should not be used for purposes of individual grading. The same is true of a department or placement test when the student does not know *in advance* what is being tested and how it is being tested.

When should tests such as those developed by textbook authors be used? If they are not criterion-referenced tests, and most of them are not, they can be used when the student has completed the indicated chapters as a measure of what the student has learned *apart from* the objectives. They may be of mild interest to both student and teacher, but unless they are built on performance objectives known to the student in advance of the testing (and preferably in advance of the learning), they should not be used for grading purposes in a performance curriculum. John L. D. Clark, writing, in Volume 4 of the *ACTFL Review of Foreign Language Education,* states that publishers are in an "especially favorable position" to develop tests for individualized courses built upon their own materials because the content is already specified in the materials. He states that the problem of identifying test vocabulary would be the most difficult for large-scale testing organizations (Clark, 1972, pp. 228-29).

One may ask, "Should students ever be given any tests other than criterion-referenced tests for purposes of grading?" The answer is affirmative, but it rests on the premise that the student knows for what material he is responsible. He may be told that, upon completion of a set number of objectives (ten, for example), he will be asked to demonstrate the competencies gained in those ten objectives in several new ways, and the ways should be listed. Clark (1972, pp. 239-40) cautions against the use of multiple-choice tests as the sole means of testing performance objectives. He lists the chance success factor (guessing) as a major concern, and he alludes to the difficulty of constructing valid test items that measure only one linguistic feature. He suggests that spoken or written responses may provide more reliable measurement. This in essence means that the student will be given a new performance objective, but it may blend smaller objectives into a unit, and the means of demonstration may be more interesting and/or more challenging.

This writer does not believe that students should stay at low-level testing of small bits of cognitive knowledge. Such immobility makes learning dull and does not enable the learner to progress. If, on the other hand, the testing is going to be on new levels or to involve new approaches to the materials, the teacher should make up the test (at least in his mind) in advance of his teaching. Teaching should always be *directed* towards certain outcomes. This in no way limits what will occur during teaching, and, by means of an additional test, a teacher has an opportunity to build upon those vicarious experiences that have occurred while he was directing the class towards a specific objective. If, during the activities that are designed to help the student meet certain objectives, the teacher develops new directions (perhaps at student urging), the test should still be aimed at the original specific objectives, because that is what the teacher promised at the outset of the learning. However, the teacher can also choose to define a new objective and can construct a test to measure this new objective. The new test should come *after* the specific objective has been reached. The teacher may want to revamp his curriculum the following year so that the new objective replaces one of the previous year.

Some critics have argued that a series of criterion-referenced tests could lead to the mastering of a set of objectives that would be quickly forgotten. There are two solutions to this problem: one, to construct learning objectives that are sequenced and developed to lead to terminal course objectives; two, to use comprehensive random achievement monitoring (see below). If the objectives and tests are developed to lead to a high level of student performance at the end of the course, then objectives would normally increase both skill and content as the course developed. Reinforcement is needed with performance objectives, but once skill and content have been mastered, less reinforcement should be needed.

Comprehensive random achievement monitoring provides a ready means of review and testing. The teacher indicates to the student that at stated intervals he will have a test on all previous objectives. The teacher then chooses test items from a selection of previous objectives and makes a test. He can quickly determine which students have retained mastery of the objective.

The next question might be, "Who makes up the criterion-referenced test?" The answer is obvious: either the person who wrote the performance objective, or the teacher who is using the performance objective, or some third party. If the performance objective is well written so that content is specified, expected student performance is indicated, the circumstances under which the student will perform are delineated, and time limitations (if any) and the criteria of measurement are stated, *anyone* can write the test items. It is when the content area is hazy, when the skill or circumstances are ill-defined, when the criterion of measurement is not specific that confusion and pandemonium result. Teachers will in all probability be the first to construct criterion-referenced tests since they are the sole arbiters of the content of their curriculum.

Teachers have frequently shown great creativity when faced with problems. A young colleague of mine (who teaches biology)— Mr. Neil Morris of Glenbrook South High School, Glenview, Illinois—has prepared a test bank. He asked for and received test items from all his colleagues, and he prepared a number himself. He then had each item typed on a 3 x 5 card and indexed with the number of the objective it tested. For each objective, he had 10 or 20 cards. When he wished to make a test he taped selected cards to a paper, xeroxed the paper and produced a test. In this way he could produce an almost infinite number of variant tests. In the next steps he added the answers to the left edge of each card. He xeroxed this first to make an answer sheet, then covered the answers with tape, and xeroxed the student test. Obviously, a computer could be utilized most effectively in this process. Nevertheless, textbook authors and professional testing establishments such as the Educational Testing Service could well perform the task if they were working from established performance objectives. Both textbook authors and testing services hate to dictate objectives, but for years both groups have dominated teaching and learning from the sidelines. The Modern Language Achievement Tests and the Pimsleur Proficiency Tests exerted a measure of this influence when schools began administering these on a regular basis. The College Entrance Examination Board Achievement Tests and the Advanced Placement Tests have also dictated curriculum. Even the contest examinations administered by such organizations as the American Association of Teachers of French and its sister groups have had an influence on selection of texbooks, curriculum, and teaching techniques. Clever teachers quickly ascertained what the makers of the tests wished to measure, and they emphasized that particular portion of the content. Some schools have taken the position, perhaps rightly, that all these tests are at variance with their goals. If the test makers stated their performance objectives, teachers and students would be in a position to decide intelligently whether or not the test measured their particular curriculum effectively. This might of course reduce the number of people who would buy these tests, and this may be one reason why test makers seem reluctant to state their objectives. What seems more convincing, however, is that the profession as a whole is not in agreement concerning what is important in language learning, so test constructors have few guidelines or directions from a unified profession. They do rely on committees, but these committees may not always be representative of views held throughout the country.

It would seem that it is essential to define several levels of competency in the "four skills" and to indicate content areas within each. A student then could submit his competencies to a teacher, a college, or an employer. It would not be strange to have a student with a high level of listening comprehension in the areas of news and political events who might have speaking competencies only in practical "travel" vocabulary. He might have few if any writing skills. To accommodate the needs of such a student would necessitate a great revision in curricular offerings. But such a revision will be upon us anyway if we wish to keep our clientele.

One final word of caution. Many supervisors of experimental projects, and many designers of PPBS systems (see Chapter XVII), are evaluating their projects by using norm-referenced standardized tests. This is tragic, for many fine projects may be jettisoned because someone mistakenly thinks that they are not achieving adequate results. If money and funding are attached to objectives, those objectives must be measured by tests designed to measure them appropriately, not by tests that may throw in random facts that play no part in achieving the objectives listed. Language teachers must take this matter into consideration as they prepare to defend their programs and get their fair share of funding under new accountability systems. In order to measure their students' learning, teachers must be prepared to write criterion-referenced tests, to select criterion-referenced tests for measurement of objectives, and to argue eloquently against the use of inappropriate evaluation tools in measuring their programs.

For a more thorough treatment of this subject, see a short and readable book edited by W. James Popham, *Criterion-Referenced Measurement* (1971). In this volume Popham, Robert Glaser, and others discuss important concepts (such as validity, variability, reliability) relating to this type of test.

This is an age of educational innovations, and as frequently happens when new ideas begin to appear, they are often caught in the mire of traditional practices that would at first glance appear to be of little import. Nevertheless, it is such carefully entrenched institutions as the honor roll, class rank, and grading patterns that frequently curb and curtail educational innovations that could otherwise have far-reaching influence. In a day when students are calling for relevance, individuality, and open access to education, it seems ludicrous at first glance to note that a traditional pattern of grading may prevent strides from being made in any of these areas. There is an analogous inverse practice: some feel so inclined to innovate without understanding the needs or the purposes of innovation that they, hearing others condemn traditional grading practices, are wont to join in the fray with little understanding of why they are changing the current system. This, then, is one of the dilemmas of modern education: there are some who are change-happy; they will not hesitate to change anything. And there are others who cling desperately to anachronisms that perpetuate a state of inefficiency.

It may indeed be necessary for teachers to adapt a performance curriculum to the traditional grading system during the first phase. Too many changes brought about at the same time can doom them all. Let us assume that a school has an A to F grading system. How can teachers operate within it if they use performance objectives? The following procedures should prove helpful:

1. Visit the department supervisor, principal, dean, director of curriculum, assistant superintendent, or superintendent and inform him (or them) of your desire to use slightly different grading procedures. Do not forget the guidance department either. Tell them that you expect to raise student achievement and to lower or abolish failure. Show them your objectives and your criteria. Tell them that you expect to stay within the system but that you expect grades to rise. This will help to allay their fears that you may be "watering down standards."

2. Consider adopting, at the start, a modified mastery level system.
   Example A: All students are assigned the same number of objectives, but they *complete* varying numbers of objectives.

   If a student achieves all objectives to the specified level of mastery he receives an *A*.

   If the student achieves 90% of the assigned objectives to the level of mastery he receives a *B*.

   If the student achieves 80% of the assigned objectives to the level of mastery he receives a *C*.

Such a system might be used where the number of objectives is large. The teacher's own responsibility is to help all students achieve at least 80% of the objectives.

Example B: All students would have to complete all the objectives, but there would be several levels of "mastery," specified by measurement criteria (see above). This procedure most closely resembles the traditional system.

Example C: All students complete all objectives and reach a mastery level of at least a *C* or they receive a grade of "incomplete." This policy may require administrative approval.

Example D: A common level of mastery is used, but the *number* of required objectives is small. If a student achieves all the *required* objectives he receives a grade of *C.* To receive an *A* or *B* he must select and complete additional objectives from the list.

If a group pace is maintained, the grading problems will be less complex than if instruction is individualized. If all students work on the same objectives, and if all reach the same mastery level, there will be a time differential. The brighter or more highly motivated learner will complete the objectives sooner. If the objectives are the same for all, and if the time span is the same for all, chances are that the mastery levels will differ.

If an individualized system is used, however, one of the following will probably occur:

1. the students will have different objectives;
2. the students will finish at different times;
3. the students will have different levels of mastery.

For each of these options there should be a different grading system. Let us examine the three. Harry Reinert (1972, p. 96) states that in self-paced programs traditional measurements cannot be readily applied. Ideally, in individualized programs, the student should receive credit only for the work he has accomplished. This has led to two more concepts in grading procedures: differentiated credit and continuous progress.

In a continuous progress program a student *may* receive credit for the time spent in the course (such as one semester or one year), but the course is laid out on the basis of objectives, and the student begins in the fall where he left off the previous spring. Some critics might object to giving all students the same credit for achieving differing amounts of learning. Nevertheless, this is true in any school that uses ability grouping. It is also true in many colleges.

Differential credit can be applied in two different ways. If all students are assigned credit at one particular time, such as the end of a semester, then each student would receive credit for the quantity of objectives that he had achieved at that point; one student might receive 1 credit, another 3/4 of a credit, another 2/3 of a credit. The more common way of applying this principle, however, is to grant credit by semesters only, that is, for the equivalent of one semester's work. If the student does not complete the work by the end of the semester, he does not receive credit at that time, but at the time he *does* complete the work he receives his credit. Hence a student who experiences difficulties may take three semesters to complete two semesters' work, but he has no failure recorded. For obvious reasons differential credit is often not popular with school and college registrars.

No individual teacher or group of teachers, therefore, should try to implement a differential credit program without administrative approval. This type of grading and assignment of credit affects the entire school or college. It is possible to run a continuous progress program within traditional confines because grades and credit are assigned at traditional times. The only problem for the teacher is the computation of such grades.

The following guidelines might help the teacher in determining grading procedures:

1. No student who completes a set of objectives to a satisfactory mastery level should receive a grade of less than *C*.

2. Whether the stated mastery level represents an *A, B* or *C* depends on the following:
   a. number of objectives;
   b. amount of content and skill;
   c. level of mastery demanded;

3. If time is not a constraint, then a student should not be penalized in his grade for taking additional time to meet the objectives.

No matter what type of program you devise, do try to implement a testing and grading system that supports it. If you cannot change the system, implement your program in such a way that the student is fairly treated. Be sure to:

a. inform students, parents and guidance personnel of grading procedures *prior to* implementing them;

b. clear any new practices with administrators *before* announcing these to students and parents;

c. inform your *colleagues* in the department of any new grading practices and provide them with a rationale.

Your innovation may be superb, but unless it is backed by a supportive administration, unless it is understood by your colleagues, and unless it is accepted by students and parents, it may be doomed to early failure. It is much easier to plan ahead than it is to put out "bushfires" of indignation. The grading system, certainly, must be thought through before anyone implements a performance curriculum.

VIII. INDIVIDUALIZED INSTRUCTION

It is possible to develop a performance curriculum without individualizing instruction. Conversely, it is possible to individualize instruction without using performance objectives. Nevertheless, the use of performance objectives will help assure the success of any individualized program. Individualization by its very nature implies that the curriculum will not be the same for all students. Whether the teacher individualizes rate, materials, methods, content, or objectives, both the student and the teacher must clearly understand what the student is to do. As long as the student is being taught in a group, the teacher has the option of explaining and demonstrating and leading the student step by step. The student simply does what he is told. On the other hand, in an individualized program the teacher must at some time rely upon the written word or a tape or a film or a colleague to do some of the instructing. On occasion, the student selects the mode of instruction best suited to himself, or the teacher suggests materials that are compatible with the student's interests, abilities, or needs. *At all times the student must know in advance what he is supposed to be able to do when he has finished his tasks.* The simplest way to inform the student of this end product is to give him a set of performance objectives.

Howard Altman and a distinguished set of colleagues have considered practical problems that plague individualized learning programs (see Altman, 1972). A failure to plan or to plan sufficiently and a lack of classroom management lead the list of such problems. Most of these writers consider the preparation of performance objectives an essential part of the planning process. Performance objectives help the teacher and the student to know what should be accomplished, allow the teacher to design in advance activities, self-tests, and "real" tests, and help the teacher to articulate the student's progress from one level to the next.

Once the teacher has spelled out the course in performance terms, once he has indicated the skills the student must demonstrate, and once he has determined and indicated the limits of the content to be covered, then the teacher can decide *what* he will individualize. For example, he may choose rate.

If his decision is rate, he then needs to make record sheets, establish class procedures, arrange with the administration to make the grading procedures flexible, and arrange with his colleagues for articulation at the next level. He also needs to determine when the student will work individually and when he will be involved in group work.

It may be that the teacher does not choose to individualize rate but rather chooses to individualize the activities and resources. All students will be tested on the same objectives at the same time, but the *means* each student uses to reach these objectives may differ. If the system can offer him a choice of activities, the student may choose among the following: a teacher presentation, a tape, a written handout, a book, a discussion with another student, some written exercises, an oral drill session. All may offer him access to the same skills and content, but one student may learn more effectively from one resource than from another. It does not matter what resource is chosen as long as the student is ultimately able to perform at the level indicated.

Methods also may be individualized if the student knows exactly what he is to do at the end of the instruction. One student may profit from a strictly audio-lingual approach that emphasizes mimicry and memorization through repetition. Another student may profit more from a cognitive approach that explains what is happening and then provides the necessary drill. The method in and of itself is really unimportant; *what is important is what the student is able to do at the end of the instruction.* The age of pluralism teaches us that students learn in a variety of ways. "Method" is simply a means to an end; it is learning, the end product, that counts and not the input or the means of instruction.

Some teachers prefer to individualize the *expectations* for each student. They choose to leave the time factor constant. All students complete a semester of German or French, but the expectations for each student are different. How does one define these expectations? By means of performance objectives. Anyone who has taught a course in second-year French, Spanish, or German will tell you that not every student in the class is capable of performing in the same way as every other student either in terms of skills or content—even if all the students studied by the same method from the same text with the same teacher the previous year. The difficulty is that we do not always take the time to determine what each student is able to do and what he is not able to do. I remember vividly from several years ago a second-year French class in which I had spent the first four weeks reviewing the previous year's work. One student excelled during the review period. When we began the new work he obviously was having difficulty. I asked him how he had been able to perform so well during the review and yet was having such a disproportionate amount of difficulty. He answered, "Well, you see, you reviewed all the things I knew, but you did not review the things I did not know, and now we have to use many of the verbs and vocabulary words that I did not learn last year; so I have to learn all the new and all the old at once." Just as I was feeling desperate he added, "But the review did give me confidence!" Had I measured the skills in performance terms and had I specified content, I could have built a much more appropriate review that would have provided a much better bridge to the new material. It was also apparent that not all students in the class needed the same type of review. A good criterion-referenced test given at the start of the semester would have indicated what each student needed. The review could then have been personalized and built around the needs of each student. Thus, performance objectives provide the basis for diagnosing student needs and for prescribing learning—be it with objectives, resources, or activities. Personalized learning implies that the teacher knows both his subject and his students well. He minimizes the difficulties for both if he knows in advance what each student should accomplish.

Some will argue that there is no true individualization if all objectives are determined in advance. But it is unrealistic to expect teachers to create a set of objectives for each student in five classes unless the teacher has a bank of objectives from which to draw. He may indeed write some personal objectives for an individual student, but if he has suitable "mass objectives" for the greater part of the course, he will have more time to devise special objectives for the student with the unusual needs.

Students need to be exposed to many different types of objectives. In any individualized course students should be encouraged to write their own objectives. They will have difficulty doing this until they know enough about the subject to understand how the subject is structured. They can, however, be taught to skip (for them) unessential learning objectives. All learning consists of a structure of pieces or components. The problem is that students seldom see the value of each component, and indeed, for them, any one component may have no value. Individualization offers them a choice, but in order to assure that learning does take place there must be a structure, and the choice must be clearly indicated. Too many individualized projects consist of "doing your own thing." On numerous occasions teachers have found that this has meant doing nothing. *Performance objectives serve as a constant reminder of the goal to be accomplished.* If the objectives are measured at frequent intervals by criterion-referenced tests, then the individualized program should be assured a measure of success. Students enjoy a sense of accomplishment and achievement. Performance objectives provide the framework or setting in which this success can occur.

In an individualized language program it is necessary to have excellent oral performance criteria. Many individualized courses are only "cookbook" courses or "paper and pencil" courses in some teachers' minds. In language classes this should seldom be true. If we can determine the steps that lead to conversation (see Chapter IX) we should be able to delineate performance objectives that each student can meet. Most students are interested in being able to speak a language. They should know that learning objectives are expected, and they should have materials that will help them reach these objectives. These objectives should lead the student to speaking skills. We should not expect students to learn to speak in isolation.

Individualization in no way implies that the student must work alone—at least not all the time or even most of the time. For conversational purposes students need to have access to small groups so that they can practice speaking in a realistic setting.

Some time ago, when my husband and I were planning a trip to Greece, I was given a recording to help me learn modern Greek. I approached this task with great glee. At first I heard a voice say in English, "Good morning," then the Greek equivalent; next I heard, "Good evening" and then the Greek equivalent; there followed "Good night" and "Hello," then came "I should like to have an appointment with Mr. Pergakes at three o'clock on Monday afternoon." I could not help thinking how unrealistic this was in performance terms. The neophyte can seldom move from such short and simple phrases to complex sentences. The affective domain is shattered because all the confidence the student has built up is destroyed. Some good work in performance objective writing would have helped the author of the recorded materials to create a more realistic learning situation.

To sum up: in an individualized program, performance objectives serve to accomplish the following:

a. They state to student and teacher what the outcome of the learning should be;

b. They provide a base for individualizing rate, activities, methods, resources and/or objectives;

c. They provide a basis for diagnosing student learning needs and prescribing learning objectives, activities, and resources;

d. They provide a means for assessing whether areas such as conversational skills are adequately covered.

As such, performance objectives seem to be a necessary part of the planning and organization of individualized foreign language programs.

IX. CONVERSATIONAL SKILLS

Every foreign language teacher (with rare exception) wants his students to learn to speak the foreign language. Indeed this became a national goal with the advent of Sputnik and the avalanche of NDEA institutes, audio-lingual methods, etc. No one denies the validity of the goal. The truth is, however, that a decade and a half after Sputnik, we have not nearly attained that goal, although we do have many pieces of the puzzle. Our teachers are by and large linguistically more competent in the area of speaking. We have materials that should help the student to acquire a speaking proficiency, and we have highlighted the importance of speaking. We should recognize these gains and be proud of them. Nevertheless, one must admit that we have learned more about how to get a student to repeat than how to inspire him to initiate. We now know more about how to provoke him to memorize dialogues than we do about how to teach him to generate speech. We know more about how to help him present material than we know about how to help him interact with others. The fact is that we teachers have seldom confronted the art of speaking and conversing directly. We have not examined the components and broken them down into attainable performance objectives. We have not assigned responsibility to the several levels for the various skills of speaking as we have for the various facets of structure. This chapter will present one view about how conversational skills can be structured via performance objectives and how these objectives can be distributed in a four-year sequence. Obviously other teachers could devise different systems to meet their individual needs more effectively.

The following skills are needed if one is to converse with others with some degree of fluency:

a. Answering (either questions or statements);
b. combining ideas (this may be supportive, contrastive, or provocative);
c. restating ideas;
d. questioning;
e. commenting;
f. initiating;
g. presenting;
h. interacting.

Of the above-listed skills, only two—answering and presenting—are covered in most curricula. To be sure, restatement is used sometimes in the early stages of language learning, but it is seldom developed as a conversational skill. Even answering, the most highly developed of the skills, is frequently left on a low plane; the student answers in level IV the same type of question that he answered in level II; the only new component is the content.

What I propose, then, is to structure these skills into a four-year curriculum which introduces them all in the first level and re-enters them all throughout the four years, while highlighting or accenting each in turn at an appropriate level. Let us look first at a chart of the areas of responsibility and accentuation:

Answering	Level I
Combining	Level II
Restating	Level I
Questioning	Levels I and II
Commenting	Levels II and III
Initiating	Level III
Presenting	Level IV
Interacting	Levels III and IV

As stated above, all skills would be utilized at all levels, but special emphasis could be placed as indicated. Level I would then have the specific responsibility for emphasizing the skills of answering, restating, and questioning. It is a sad commentary that we teach students to answer questions beautifully, but when they travel they need to know how to *ask* questions much more than they need to know how to *answer* them. Also, if students learn early how to ask questions the teacher can assume less of a dominant role in the class and can give the students more opportunity to speak with one another. The teacher can then assume the role of listener, re-inforcer, and guider of the conversation groups. Especially in the beginning, however, the teacher must assume the leadership role. Let us take a simple lesson in French level I to show how these skills can be taught via performance objectives:

Objective I The student will answer simple questions using the verb *aller* when shown visuals of the beach and the market place. These questions will use the questioning words *où* (where) and *qui* (who).

Teacher gives Marie a picture of the market place and

asks Marie:	*Où vas-tu?*
Marie answers:	*Je vais au marché.*

Teacher gives Jean a picture of the beach and

asks Jean:	*Où vas-tu?*
Jean answers:	*Je vais à la plage*
Teacher asks Pierre:	*Qui va à la plage?*

Pierre sees Jean holding the picture

and answers:	*Jean va à la plage*
Teacher asks Ludvig:	*Qui va au marché?*
Ludvig answers:	*Marie va au marché.*
Teacher asks Chantal:	*Où va Jean?*
Chantal replies:	*Jean va à la plage.*
Teacher asks Robert:	*Où va Marie?*
Robert answers:	*Marie va au marché.*

This is where many teachers would stop; perhaps there would have been some choral repetition, but the lesson would end there. Let us see how we could proceed at the act of combining:

Teacher asks Marie:	*Tu va à la plage?*
Marie answers:	*Non, Madame, je vais au marché mais,*
	Jean va à la plage.
Teacher asks Jean:	*Tu vas à la plage?*
Jean replies:	*Oui, Madame, je vais à la plage mais*
	Marie va au marché.

Teacher says:	*Dis cela à Marie.*
Jean follows:	*Marie, tu vas au marché mais je vais à la plage.*
Marie answers:	*Oui, tu vas à la plage mais je vais au marché.*
Teacher asks Pierre:	*Qui va à la plage et qui va au marché?*
Pierre answers:	*Jean va à la plage et Marie va au marché.*

We have now encountered the next conversational skill: restatement. Let us admit that all beginning lessons are somewhat repetitious because we want to have the students reach the objective of answering; at this point content is less important than process. Certainly the teacher would assume that the students Marie, Jean, and Pierre could answer simple questions; nevertheless, assumption is not enough. The teacher would have to give each student a chance to demonstrate his competency by answering the simple questions. Then the students would be asked to reach Performance Objective 2 (below).

Objective 2 The student will answer compound questions using the verb *aller* when shown visuals of the beach and the market place.

Objective 3 The student will contrast his own action with that of another student in the class by making a statement to that student concerning where he is going (to the beach or to the market place) and contrasting it with where the other student is going.

This objective is crucial since the skill of conversation involves *I* and *you* and *you* and *we* quite frequently. Yet most of the restatement we teach is in the third person. This objective also forces one student to talk to another student; so he acquires the habit of conversing with someone other than the teacher. As the student acquires more competency in subject matter he can make more free responses and can generate more contrastive statements. He is now ready for the next stage in the building of his conversational skills.

Objective 4 The student will restate a contrastive statement in the third person. These statements will involve the verb *aller* and visuals of the market place and the beach.

Teacher hands visual of the beach to Jean and visual of the market place to Marie. She says nothing but points to Pierre who says:

Il va à la plage mais elle va au marché.

Please note that we have advanced several lessons and that the student has now learned the subject pronouns in the third person. Teacher then hands visuals to other students and points to a third person who makes appropriate contrastive statements. This leads to the next skill.

Objective 5 The student will initiate four (4) questions involving the verb *aller* and the market place and the beach. He will ask them of a classmate.

Teacher now leaves the visuals in the hands of students, Marie and Jean respectively, and points to Chantal who asks one of the following questions:

> *Qui va à la plage?*
> *Qui va au marché?*
> *Où va Jean?*
> *Où va Marie?*
> *Marie va à la plage?*
> *Marie va au marché?*
> *Jean va à la plage?*
> *Jean va au marché?*
> *Tu vas à la plage?*
> *Tu vas au marché?*

Chantal asks her question of another student who answers her; then the teacher points to a third student who initiates a different question. This is how the skill functions in a group.

When the student is being tested, he is frequently tested with another student so that he may interact, combine statements, and ask questions. He may see the visuals in the hands of a third and fourth student. He now must show that he can initiate four different questions. This gives him some flexibility and sets the stage for him to begin a conversation with another person even if the conversation is on a very elementary level.

One of the most exciting aspects of conversation is commenting. Students love this particular skill and engage in it frequently—at times to the detriment of the class and lesson. We should capitalize on this seemingly innate tendency by building commenting objectives into our classes. Students like to show their feelings, and if we involve them in the class by giving them an opportunity to show their reactions we provide them with skills needed to interact with others.

Objective 6 The student will make a statement to or ask a question of another student. He will follow this statement or question by a comment.

The teacher hands the visuals back to Marie and Jean.

Marie looks at Jean and says:	*Tu vas à la plage? Quelle chance!*
Jean looks at Marie and says:	*Tu vas au marché. Quel dommage!*

Comments are spicy, caustic, and/or on occasion provoking. The teacher can have real fun selecting students who will enliven otherwise dreary dialogues and conversations. Once more note that in this objective the student is talking to another student.

Up to this point we have limited ourselves to one verb (and only three or four forms of that) and two nouns. This was to show how simply the skills could be put into objectives. In the world of reality we must deal with re-entry. We cannot assume that skills taught on one day last forever; we need to review and reuse vocabulary that the student has already studied. Let us now assume a later time in the school year. The student has studied weather expressions and the negative. He has learned some new vocabulary, some commenting words, and some questioning words. He has also studied time expressions. Now we come to the initiating objectives.

Objective 7 The student will state today's weather and will ask a classmate a question like one of the following involving the verb *aller* and the market place or the beach.

Marie:	*Aujourd'hui il pleut. Tu vas à la plage?*
	Aujourd'hui il fait beau. Tu vas au marché?
	Aujourd'hui il ne fait pas beau. Tu vas à la plage?
	Aujourd'hui il fait beau. Qui va à la plage?

Since the weather is changeable this objective should be utilized whenever the teacher feels that a new situation will present itself. This objective has an additional merit since it is built on a day-to-day situation that is real to the world of conversation, namely, the weather.

This objective leads quite naturally to the skill of presenting. Many students dread third- or fourth-year language classes because after years of answering teachers' questions they suddenly have to make presentations before the class. They do not have confidence in their pronunciation, in the content they are presenting, or in their ability to present. They have had little experience in making presentations;

thus they face several unknowns. If, on the other hand, they were taught in level I to make simple presentations, this task would not seem so formidable later.

Objective 8 The student will make four statements about the weather and his plans for the day. He will use the verb *aller* and the market place and the beach.

Pierre:

Aujourd'hui il pleut. Il ne fait pas beau. Je ne vais pas à la plage. Maman veut des légumes. Je vais au marché.

Perhaps the skill of interacting will be above the achievement level of some first-level students. If, however, interacting objectives are kept very simple and if they are limited to two interactions, most first-level students can reach them.

Objective 9 The student will make a comment about the weather and will follow the comment with a question which he will ask a classmate. When the classmate answers his question the first student will follow the answer with another question. The classmate will answer this question; then the first student may pose a second question to his classmate.

Marie:

Comme il pleut aujourd'hui! Tu vas à la plage?

Jean:

Mais oui. Je veux nager. Où vas-tu?

Marie:

Je vais au marché. Maman veut des légumes. Quand vas-tu à la plage?

While this conversation is not very sophisticated, nevertheless the student is on his way to learning to react to those around him—his classmates. It is rare that we can import enough natives into the classroom to have one for the use of each student. We can, however, teach students in pairs, or in small groups, so that they acquire the custom of talking to one another, and that is the essence of conversation.

If conversational objectives are realistically structured so that students can achieve them, both the students and the teacher will experience a sense of accomplishment. It is not realistic to expect *all* the above skills to be applied *by every student* to large bodies of content material. In selecting conversation and composition objectives, teachers must strike a balance between skills and content. The "productive skills" require more time to master; once the student has mastered them, new blocks of content can be learned more readily. Please note, too, that only one tense of one verb was used throughout these examples. It is not this author's intention to suggest that only one verb be utilized throughout the objectives of the first level; it *is* my intention to show that conversational skills can be demonstrated with a minimum of content. In any event the content should be specified with each objective. Then teacher, student, parent, or administrator can tell whether the student has met the objectives. Teachers should then no longer have to endure: "But I thought he was going to learn to speak the language, and when we went to Mexico last summer, he couldn't even bargain with the taxi driver. What are you people teaching in that school anyway?"

X. TEACHING COMPOSITION

In language teaching the word "composition" has many connotations. College courses entitled "Conversation and Composition" are frequently found in catalogs. The student who enrolls in such a course may find himself memorizing lists of idioms and answering questions for the "conversation" portion and may also find that "composition" consists of translating series of tricky sentences from English into German, French, or Spanish. The older textbooks, both college and high school levels, also tended to label translation exercises "composition". Even today it is not uncommon to find many teachers hesitant to teach composition because they themselves have had little or no training in this area. For purposes of this discussion the word "composition" will mean the generating of thoughts centered around a particular topic. The composition may be "guided," that is, the teacher may supply specific guidelines that help the student, but the student must be allowed to choose the way he will express the thoughts.

Conversation and composition are two closely allied skills, although it is true that formal composition may require a different register of language. Few doctoral dissertations are written in ordinary conversational registers. Nevertheless, both skills require the generation of thoughts, the clothing of those thoughts in words and in structure, and the organizing of those thoughts. While it is true that composition most closely resembles the conversational skill discussed in the previous chapter, nevertheless, we are frequently required to use composition skills in filling out questionnaires, in providing information to others, and in answering a series of questions. Both conversation and composition require the learner to have control of vocabulary, structure, organization, content, and mechanics. In conversation the area of mechanics centers around pronunciation, accent, rhythm, and intonation; in composition, spelling, form, and punctuation are mechanical concerns that are absent in speaking. Both skills demand some talent for word choice; both require that the person generating language have something to say.

There has been much discussion, nonetheless, among foreign language teachers about the teaching of writing. To some, writing means copying and spelling. To others, writing means recording on paper what someone else says, e.g., a *dictée*. Some teachers assume that students can write if they can fill in the blanks with the correct form of the verb, others assume that the student can write if he can translate sentences from English into the target language. Many teachers would agree that the writing skill they most desire for their students is the ability to express one's thoughts in writing; they would agree that all the other forms of writing mentioned above exist as preparatory activities to help produce this skill. Yet as with conversational skills, teachers tend to jump from the lower levels of writing to "free composition," and both they and their students are frustrated when the student is unable to perform. In the pages that follow we will examine how the teaching of composition can be structured into specific performance objectives that lead to the skill of free composition.

If a student is introduced to the four skills, that is to say, unless he has elected a pure "reading approach" to the language, he should acquire some knowledge of phonics before attempting to write. If he is familiar with the principles of phonics in the target language, he will be better able to translate the sounds and words he hears into the appropriate written symbols. In free composition spelling is important; perhaps it is not the most important element, but it is needed. If a student learns to hear a sound correctly, and if he learns to spell that sound correctly, then when he reads he will automatically read the sound correctly, and he should transfer that sound correctly into writing. As with most skill development, the skill of spelling takes time. Many teachers feel obliged to teach all the elements of phonics in one year, when, in reality, most students cannot absorb all the principles so quickly. These same students did not accomplish this with their own language, and they most certainly will not do so with a second language. Some happy medium must be achieved.

That happy medium should involve the most significant elements of phonics. In learning Spanish, French, and German, therefore, since the vowels are the most critical to mastery, it is to the vowels that the teacher of the first level must initially turn. But the challenge to the English-speaking beginner varies even among these languages, for their vowel systems differ a great deal from each other. It is no secret, for example, that, of the three, French possesses the vowel system which offers the greatest difficulties to the English-speaking student. It follows, therefore, that while performance objectives dealing with spelling in general (and vowels in particular) should appropriately appear among the writing objectives for the first level in each language, those spelling objectives for level I would certainly differ from language to language in keeping with the relative levels of their phonic difficulty.

A spelling objective for Spanish level I, for example, might be:

> The student will spell correctly all vowel sounds in any word dictated, whether or not he has previously studied the word. The word will be spoken twice by the teacher. Criterion: 80%

This objective would be most unrealistic if the student were expected to take a dictation in which he would have to concentrate on comprehension elements. It would also be unrealistic if he were expected to achieve that level of mastery on the consonants. The entire objective would probably be unrealistic for a first-year French student. The French vowel system is so much more complicated that an appropriate objective would have to be more limited, viz.:

> 1. The student will spell correctly the following vowel sounds in words which he has studied: [y, e, ɛ, i, o, u.]. The teacher will speak each word twice.
> Criterion: 80%

2. The student will spell correctly the following vowel sounds in words which he may not have previously studied: [y, i, a] . The teacher will speak each word three times.

Criterion: 70%

If the curriculum contained a list of specific performance objectives in the area of spelling, and if spelling were taught as a separate skill, student mastery in this area would rise. If throughout four years of study a student gradually encountered the increasing difficulties of the phonetic system of a language, many students would not be defeated by the demand that they grasp meaning, thoughts, and mechanics at one time. Teachers would also derive increasing satisfaction from seeing that students improved their spelling proficiency year after year.

While it is crucial that the student who wishes to learn to write study and learn how to spell the new language, it is also apparent that he must not be discouraged from writing because he is unable to spell everything accurately in the early stages. One look at any writing that most students do in their own language should convince teachers that the student can indeed express his thoughts without having acquired mastery of spelling. This is difficult for many language teachers to accept since they themselves are usually good spellers, often better spellers than their counterparts in other disciplines. They also were probably taught by those who could not accept any divergence from perfection in spelling. To change this attitude will require some effort. Nevertheless, when a student converses, he may make mistakes in pronunciation, structure, accent, and when he writes, he may make mistakes in spelling, mechanics, and structure. I am not suggesting that these mistakes do not need correcting; I am suggesting that in Level I, spelling need not be the determining factor in grades *when composition is the area considered.*

If a student is to learn to express thoughts in the target language, he must begin in the early stages of language study. *He does not need a large amount of content in order to express thoughts.* It is better for him to generate a small amount of material over which he has some control. It is not necessary for him to be able to write every word that he reads or hears. It is also not necessary for him to be able to write every word that he can say. He should write those words which he has studied in some concentrated way, especially those words that he has learned to spell. One of the simplest learning objectives in the area of writing could be:

> The student will write answers to six written questions about the weather and about going to the beach and to the market place. He will use only the present tense. The answers must be appropriate to the weather of the day. Criterion: 80% of content and no more than two spelling errors. e.g.,
>
> a. *Quel temps fait-il aujourd'hui?*
> b. *Qui va à la plage?*
> c. *Pourquoi?*
> d. *Qui va au marché?*
> e. *Pourquoi?*
> f. *Où vas-tu?*

Obviously this objective is at a very low level, but the student still provides answers and generates thoughts. This type of objective is realistic in the first semester of high school language study.

Since the skills of composition and conversation are closely intertwined it would be advisable to have the student practice orally some of the topics on which he might later write compositions. Most first-year students study topics such as the family, pets, vacations, etc., and these provide good topics for short one-paragraph compositions. As with spelling, there must be some leeway shown in teaching the organization of the paragraph. The student will not normally absorb this by osmosis. He must be taught. Nevertheless, the first task is to get him to generate several sentences about a topic and to write these sentences on paper!

> Make five statements about your family. You may consider ideas such as: the number of sisters and brothers that you have, the age of your grandmother or grandfather, your father's profession, a description of your brothers, sisters, or parents. You may also consider any pets as members of the family and may add statements about them.
> Criterion: 80% of the statements should be correct as to content.

Obviously the teacher could add other elements such as spelling errors or grammatical areas to the criterion. He could also add to the circumstances that the student would not be allowed to make more than two statements of the same type such as, "I have two brothers." Some students will make all five statements about one aspect of the family, for instance, age. They all love to tell their mother's age!

Notice that no organization for the paragraph is called for in the objective. It is not that organization is considered unimportant, but it is necessary to solve one problem at a time. If the student can learn to generate five statements about a specific subject, he can then be taught to organize those statements into a paragraph.

If one wishes to teach organization, the following objective may prove useful:

> When given five sentences in German about your school, you will rearrange the sentences to form a cohesive paragraph. You will indicate which sentence is the topic sentence. If there is no topic sentence you will write one.
> Criterion: 80% of the sentences will be properly arranged.

Again, no mention of spelling or writing errors was made. The student has the five sentences before him. Organization, not spelling, is the primary concern. He may have some difficulty writing the topic sentence. He should not, however, be preoccupied with other concerns.

A word of caution is needed here. We are speaking of first-level writing skills. If the same type of assignment were given in second level, I would require a higher level of mastery particularly in the area of spelling, since the student would presumably have mastered more of the spelling principles of the language.

If the above objectives formed part of a set of learning objectives, an appropriate *terminal* course objective could be:

> You will write a short paragraph in class on one of the following topics (to be selected by your teacher): the school, the weather, your family, your vacation, what you eat for breakfast and dinner, going to the beach. Your composition will be evaluated on:
>
> | Content | (Does it make sense?); |
> |---|---|
> | Organization | (Does it have a topic sentence and a concluding sentence?); |
> | Spelling | (Not more than three errors). |
>
> You may not use notes, book, etc.

By the time a student moves into level II he should be accustomed to arranging his thoughts around a topic and recording those thoughts in writing. In level II he will probably work with short reading assignments. He can be asked to make statements about what he has read. It is preferable for him to do this orally first, especially in the learning stages. Then he can be asked to do some form of the following objective:

> You will read in class a short passage (one page) based on one of following topics: the French *lycée,* Christmas in France, or a tour of Versailles. You will then answer in writing (using complete sentences) ten questions in French based on the passage.
>
> Criterion: Nine correct content answers.
> No more than two spelling errors.
> No more than three grammatical errors.

The student must demonstrate two skills here, the skill of reading comprehension and the skill of writing. One could substitute listening to a tape just as well. Nevertheless, *most students who acquire writing proficiency will also wish to acquire reading proficiency,* although the reverse is not true. The above objective has been kept relatively simple since this may be the first time the student has written answers to a reading passage which he has not seen previously. This learning objective also helps the student develop a skill that can be used in testing.

A further development toward the free composition skill occurs when the student is asked to do the following:

> You will read a short passage (one page) based on one of the following topics: the French *lycée,* Christmas in France, or a tour of Versailles. You will then summarize in one paragraph (six sentences) the main ideas expressed in the passage. Your composition will be evaluated on:
>
> Summary   (Did you choose the main ideas?);
> Organization   (Is your paragraph well organized?);
> Spelling, Grammar, (Did you make more than five errors?).
>   and Mechanics

Summarizing is a difficult art. The student is tempted to restate what is in the entire passage. That is why the summary should be limited. Summarizing also includes selection. As a learning objective to the one mentioned above, the following might serve:

> You will read a paragraph about French sports. You will then be given ten statements which might be used in a summary. Select five of the ten and arrange them in order to form both a good paragraph and a good summary.
>
> Criterion: 80%

If the student can learn to summarize in the second year, he can learn to express his opinions in the third year. In order to do the latter he needs control of various verb tenses. He also needs to be guided in the use of key words and key expressions in each language. If he has learned how to restate in first- and second-year work, i.e., how to say, "I see that . . . ," "I believe that . . . ," he then can be taught to use such expressions as "It is my opinion that . . . ," "It seems that . . . ," "People say that . . . ," "I disagree with . . . ," "Unamuno states that . . . ," etc. To develop responsibility he must learn to use facts to support his generalizations. This can come in the second stage of development if the teacher wishes. Good third-year objectives center around some controversial issue over which the student expresses an opinion in writing. It is expressly important here that he have discussed this orally so that he will have control of the vocabulary and not range too far afield in his discussion. This is a good time to use the guided composition approach:

> You will express your opinions pro or con whether the school day should be lengthened or shortened.
>
> You will consider such items as the following:
>
> The disadvantages of shortening or lengthening the school day;
> The advantages of shortening or lengthening the school day;
> The people who would be affected by the shortening or lengthening of the day;
> How our school day compares in length with that of other neighboring schools;
> Your opinion and the reasons for arriving at that opinion.
>
> Your theme may be one or two paragraphs in length. It will be evaluated on the following:
>
> The arguments you express (Are they valid? Supported by fact?);
> The organization you use (Is it logical? Convincing?);
> The language and expressions you use in presenting your arguments (Are your words aptly chosen? Are the expressions vivid? Convincing?).

In meeting this type of objective the student will frequently make errors in spelling and grammar. He becomes much more personally involved in this type of argumentative writing. He is also preoccupied with his own opinions. This may be an appropriate time to relax the demands in other areas.

If we are later to ask the student to express his opinions on governments, cultures, and works of literature, we must first teach him to express himself on topics that pertain very much to his own life. Most students are interested in themselves. They are very interested in giving their opinions on almost anything. This helps make the writing objectives relevant to the student, and a creative teacher can vary the topics so that the student is developing skills while dealing with topics of interest to him.

It is at this point that the student is most capable of writing a letter to a pen pal in the pen pal's language. I believe that first- and second-year students should have pen pals. They should be encouraged to write at least briefly each time in the pen pal's language, while by the third year they can probably express themselves at some length on a topic of their own choosing in that language. They should also encourage the pen pal to try his or her hand at responding in English. In this way both receive some practice in writing as well as in reading the foreign language. Teachers may not yet have succeeded in developing the art of writing with students who acquire pen pals in the first two years, but nevertheless many of these relationships flourish, and the students enjoy them. If the teacher capitalizes on the letter writing, the art of composition becomes much more meaningful.

By level IV the student should be developing some analytical skills. He should already be able to read, to summarize, to express his opinions. Now he needs to probe, to discuss what others have said, to note the techniques they have used, to interpret the effect that has been produced. Not all students will apply these skills to literature. Nevertheless, most students who pursue a foreign language will deal with its literature or with its people's history, economics, sociology, etc. If the student has any choice as to whether or not to write, he will probably want to write in some one area by the time he is a senior. If he has any inclination towards independent study, he must use writing at some time or other to express his findings. It is possible that at this level the student needs a voice in the type of skill he will develop. The following are offered as some suggested objectives that various types of students might select for level IV:

1. You will write a business letter to Mr. Alvarez Mendoza in Caracas. You are trying to sell Mr. Mendoza a particular type of machine that you are manufacturing, and you know that he has some interest in the machine. However, he has informed you that he is also looking at the model made by one of your competitors. Put together a fact sheet on the two

machines. You may utilize any magazines, personal contacts, commercial descriptions, etc. to obtain the facts. Then basing your letter on the two sets of data, analyze why your machine will better meet the needs of your customer.

Write a two-page letter in which you convince him that he should indeed purchase the machine that you are manufacturing. Your letter will be evaluated upon the strength of your arguments, the use of the facts in bolstering the arguments, the organizational plan you use in setting forth your arguments, the form and expressions you use in writing the letter, the correctness of grammar and style. You will write this letter out of class, and you may consult any dictionary, grammar book, resource person, etc. that you wish.

2. Compare and contrast the characters *doña Perfecta* and *doña Bárbara* from the novels of the same name. In what ways are these ladies similar? In what ways do they differ? How does each affect the outcome of the novel? Is there, in your opinion, any symbolism embodied in either character? Write a four-page essay (in Spanish, of course) in which you express your opinions on the above topics, but be sure that you support your opinion by referring to incidents in the books. Your essay will be evaluated on the analysis you make of the novel, the strength of your arguments, the quantity and quality of supporting evidence that you cite, the organization of the essay and the correctness of mechanics.

Please note that in the above objectives the acceptable number of errors was not stated, since it is frequently difficult to state at what point an essay is no longer acceptable. I prefer to ask the student to rewrite an essay that is unacceptable in terms of mechanics. Nevertheless, in a business letter a student must not make errors, for he will not be successful if he does. There is also a formalized style to business letter writing which students can learn to a fair level of proficiency, whereas style presents more difficult problems when the student writes a literary analysis. I personally tend to be very liberal in grading such themes and try rather to teach the student to rewrite. Nevertheless, others may feel quite differently. If so, they should state this in their criteria for evaluation.

Grammatical errors are another source of concern to teachers of composition. If the student has studied grammar for two or three years, the teacher might base any further study upon the errors students make in composition. If the more common errors were recorded on a transparency, flashed on the overhead projector, and corrected, the students would have an opportunity to learn from their mistakes. If the teacher followed this with a brief presentation or review of the structures, and if he then assigned some written drill material or a short, one-paragraph, guided composition, the student would find the lesson relevant because it is connected to errors that he has made. The mastery level for these particular constructions can then be much higher. In short, the teacher can devise some additional composition objectives as he teaches the course.

Many of the critics of performance objectives state that it is impossible to predict every element of evaluation, and they imply that it is therefore of little use to state any of the devices used in evaluation. I contend that it helps the student to know the focus of the essay in advance. If he knows the main emphasis, if he understands that at a certain point in learning a specific level of mastery may be acceptable which will no longer be acceptable at a more advanced point in learning, then he will know better how to proceed.

Composition, then, is an intricate and complex art. It may not be suitable for everyone, but that is not to say that anyone who is willing to spend the time and energy learning the skills may not be able to express his thoughts in some coherent state. The problems that have emerged in the past center around a vague notion as to what composition actually is—whether it is translation, answering questions, or generating new material. These problems have also centered around the objectives that have been too complex for many students in the class. It seems to me that this is the part of the curriculum that can be the most easily individualized. Most composition work is done outside of class; if the teacher has a list of five possible performance objectives for students in the area of composition, he and each student together can determine which objective the student is able to meet. Then the student with high ability is not held back by the student who is unable to meet the objective, and the student with less ability in this area is not discouraged by having to admit that he cannot reach the objective. It may be that some students should have *no* objectives in the area of composition. The teacher and the student may come to this conclusion. If so, the student may spend his time perfecting other language skills. If learning is a life-long process, this student may feel more comfortable attempting composition at some future date. Until that time, however, he will not be able to engage in those courses that demand composition skills. This is a situation in which the teacher must be both honest and kind to the student, for never is a teacher more of a guidance counselor than when he helps the student to elect and meet objectives which are both realistic and rewarding.

To sum up: The student will learn to write with less suffering if the writing objectives are organized in the following way:

1. Spelling objectives are separate objectives at least in levels I and II;
2. spelling objectives *per se* have a relatively high mastery level;
3. spelling level in compositions is not at a high mastery level;
4. the student is asked to generate thoughts in writing in level I;
5. organization is taught and evaluated separately in levels I and II;
6. writing objectives are organized in a sequential pattern from level I through levels IV and V;
7. various writing skills such as summarizing, synthesizing, analyzing, and expressing opinions are taught through specific performance objectives;
8. at levels III-V grammar or structure is taught functionally, i.e., the teacher bases the grammar lessons upon mistakes the student has made in the area of composition.

While the above principles may not assure each student success, they should help each develop a measure of proficiency in the area of composition.

XI. LISTENING COMPREHENSION

There are few experiences more rewarding in foreign language study than being able to comprehend a conversation, a radio broadcast, a television program, or a film. Yet relatively few Americans acquire a competency that permits these enjoyments. There is a wide gap between comprehending schoolroom French, Spanish, German, or Russian and understanding that of the native country. Much effort has been expended to bridge the gap, but as with the other skills there have been few programs devoted exclusively to developing the art of listening comprehension. For one thing we have tried to keep listening comprehension at the same level of competency as speaking and writing. This is a grave error, for listening is a receptive skill like reading, and hence develops at a different, faster rate than speaking and writing. This is in no way to deny that listening requires very real competencies that must be developed. A series of realistic performance objectives at every level of the curriculum, or indeed a course or mini-course devoted exclusively to listening comprehension, can help students develop these talents.

Listening comprehension objectives can begin during the early weeks of language study. The student must understand what he is saying. If he is to memorize a dialogue it is wise to have him listen to the dialogue, then study the explanation of it, then listen to the dialogue again. The first learning objective might center around the dialogues or passages being studied:

> The student will listen to isolated sentences from the dialogue and will correctly indicate the meaning of the individual sentence by selecting the appropriate picture or English counterpart. Criterion: five out of six correct.

After the student has studied four or five dialogues he may proceed to another learning objective:

> The student will listen to recombinations of the four dialogues studied. He will then indicate the meaning of ten isolated sentences by selecting the appropriate English counterpart from the list provided.
> Criterion: eight out of ten correct.

During the early weeks the student should also be taught classroom directions. The teacher can thereby brighten many otherwise mundane classroom conversations by conducting them in the foreign language. An objective appropriate to this stage of learning is:

> When given directions such as "Open your book," "Take out a piece of paper," "Turn to page 10," "Close the window," and others from the list attached, the student will carry out these directions by performing the activities indicated.
> Criterion: ten out of ten correct.

Teachers should talk to students in the foreign language. They should tell them simple stories or anecdotes. They should also have students listen to these on tapes or on records. These stories or anecdotes should primarily contain known vocabulary, particularly in the early weeks. After telling the story the teacher should ask four or five oral questions and should let students volunteer for the answers. Then the following objective would be appropriate:

> Your teacher will recount to you once, for three minutes, an incident that happens in your classroom or in your school. She will then ask you five questions in French about the incident. You will select the correct picture or English sentence that most appropriately answers the question.
> Criterion: four out of five correct.

If the student becomes accustomed to hearing his teacher tell stories, read stories, or tell anecdotes, he will easily adapt to hearing these on a tape. If he has already had the experience of identifying the various sentences from dialogues he has studied on a tape, the tape will not frighten him. Most of our tapes in foreign language study contain material that is in the textbook or workbook. This is not what *should* occur. On the tape there should be material which is new to the student at least in form. After the first six or seven weeks, some cognates should find their way into these tapes. The student should listen to the tape recorded by a native speaker; then he should hear a series of questions; next he should indicate the answers on an answer sheet. He should then check his answers. If he has understood the general thrust of the passage, he may want to work at recording it in *dictée* form. When he has had this type of experience the student is ready for the following objective:

> You will listen to a three-minute tape recorded at moderate speed by a native speaker. The tape will contain vocabulary which you have studied recently (on the list attached). You will hear the tape once. Then you will hear seven questions in Spanish. You will select the answers to the questions from the pictures or English counterparts on your answer sheets. Criterion: five out of seven correct.

There are many useful lessons that can be learned from areas such as values clarification. All of us like to express our opinions about many topics. In the early stages of language learning the student is frequently unable to express many of his thoughts because he does not have sufficient control over vocabulary, structure, or speech habits. He can, however, participate in activities such as the following:

The teacher asks a question in the foreign language such as:

How many of you like	to go to the beach?
	to go to the movies?
	to do your homework?
	to visit your relatives?
	to play with your dog?
	to study for tests?
Do you prefer	to ski or to swim?
	to study or to watch television?
	to read or to listen to a tape?
	to listen to the teacher explain a
	lesson or to read it yourself?

The student raises a hand if the question (or the alternative) matches his tastes or interests. All students can participate in this activity.

It helps to get them involved; it helps set the stage for conversation groups, and it is an excellent way to train the ear in a foreign language. If the teacher spends five minutes three times a week asking a series of prepared or spontaneous questions, the students will soon become accustomed to the practice. The teacher can insert some topics that are purely local in interest but which might also tell him how the class is reacting to the subject. This is an excellent way to seed vocabulary which the teacher may hope to introduce in a more formal way at a later date. The technique could also be used for measuring student attitudes at various points during the course. A performance objective such as the following could emerge:

> You will listen to twenty questions asking whether or not you like certain sports or activities, whether you prefer the one to the other. You will mark your responses on the answer sheet. Then you will write in English a short summary of what you put on the answer sheet.
> Criterion: twelve out of twenty responses correctly recorded in the English summary.

Radio or television commercials provide a wonderful opportunity for students to practice listening comprehension. They may already have some familiarity with the product being advertised. Since commercials are frequently repeated and since they contain much redundancy, they are a good place for the student to begin hearing the language as it is heard by natives. These commercials can be taped. If the student has worked with live material he can be asked to do the following:

> Listen to the following commercial three times. Then select all the slogans or pictures that are mentioned in the commercial. There are ten correct answers.
> Criterion: seven out of ten correct.

If a student can reach the above-mentioned objectives at the end of his first year of language study he will be on his way to acquiring proficiency in listening comprehension. Notice that in all of the above objectives the student was demonstrating his listening proficiency by indicating pictures or English counterparts. He did not have to read or write the target language in order to indicate comprehension. In an individualized program, most students can reach listening objectives, but many are unable to reach speaking, writing, or reading objectives so rapidly. The listening objectives provide them with a level of achievement that may equal that of their more talented peers.

Professor Edward D. Allen of Ohio State University, has utilized taped interviews with students in France and in Mexico to teach listening comprehension. He flashes a slide of the individual being interviewed on the screen. He then proceeds to ask questions about dating customs, summer jobs, French schools, etc. (Allen, 1974). An appropriate performance objective would be:

> Listen to a five-minute interview. Then read the questions and possible answers in the answer booklet. Indicate the correct response on your answer sheet.

The questions can appear either in English or in the target language, but if they are written in the target language, reading skills in the foreign language as well as listening comprehension are being tested.

In any program stressing the four skills it is desirable to test listening comprehension on every test or at least every major test. The *dictée* as we have mentioned previously is not necessarily a pure measure of listening comprehension; it is also a spelling test. Nevertheless, if a student learns to take dictation on a regular basis, this will help him in the area of listening comprehension, particularly in the matter of accuracy. In listening as well as in reading there are several levels. So far we have talked only of the art of receiving, as distinguished from interacting. This is a necessary first step, but the student must eventually move on.

In a curriculum that is to concentrate on speaking and listening there should also be a variety of tapes, records, films, radio broadcasts, television programs, and/or video tapes. The filmstrip and tape make excellent resources and are not as expensive as some others. Cultural lessons can be presented simply with filmstrip and tape (see Chapters XIV and XV). The student can develop his listening skills as he learns some basic facts about the people whose language he is studying. Care must be exercised, for deep cultural meaning cannot always be taught through the sole medium of the target language during the first or second year. Nevertheless, there are some areas of culture that lend themselves naturally to listening comprehension. Short (15-minute) films are excellent resources.

An appropriate performance objective would be:

You will view the following film twice. While the film is being rewound at the end of the first showing you will answer as many of the 15 questions as possible on your answer sheet *in pencil.* You will then see the film again. You may change any answers and you may answer additional questions. Record all answers you write this time *in ink.*
Criterion: 12 out of 15 correct.

An answer recorded in pencil is just as valid as an answer recorded in ink, but it tells the teacher which students need only one viewing of the film, which students do not comprehend much the first time, etc. The purpose is not to ferret out an "elite" group, but to recognize which students comprehend on one, two, or three viewings.

Conversation is often fast paced. A person must be able to respond quickly, hence he must understand what the other person is saying. An appropriate skill is to select the correct rejoinder. The student hears: "Oh, look how it is raining! We can't even get to the car!"

Rejoinder
  (a) Put the basket on the table, please.
  (b) Why don't you sit down inside and wait until it stops?
  (c) The bus stops at the corner.
  (d) I don't like eggs.

The student must comprehend the original statements, and he must select the most appropriate rejoinder. He is in the process of training his ears so that he will hear correctly what is being sent, and, at this stage, he has to select an appropriate reply. It is only a matter of time until he will be able to *generate* an appropriate reply.

It is important for the student to be exposed to live material in the early stages of learning. By live material I mean the target language as it is really spoken. If he has access to television shows, radio broadcasts, and films he will have this exposure. If not, he should hear some taped material that is recorded at normal conversational speed. He should not be expected to master this material at the first hearing. Indeed the first hearing may shock him. He should, however, hear *short* segments of live material frequently. This live material should, whenever possible, be based upon vocabulary that is known to him. The speed, the rhythm, the intonation, the junctures will intensify problems and obstacles of unknown vocabulary. Short commands such as those given on the airlines, e.g., "Fasten your seatbelts, ladies and gentlemen, and no smoking, please," are the type of material that is most appropriate. If travel vocabulary is handled in this manner, the student will have the added reinforcement of being able to comprehend directions in limited situations in the event that he has the opportunity to travel during the early stages of learning. An appropriate performance objective would be:

> Listen to the 5 sets of directions given on the tape, then write in English a short description of what you were asked to do. The tape will be run twice. All conversations will be at normal speed.
> Criterion: 4 out of 5 sets correct.

If a student elects a mini-course or a complete course in listening comprehension, he may spend most of his time listening to television shows, tapes, and films. He will begin to receive cues from sources other than the spoken language, and this is good. Native speakers of any language derive meaning from visual and tactile cues, as well as from those which are auditory. The student who acquires a high level of listening comprehension will be on the threshold of speaking. He will have learned a large quantity of passive vocabulary. As he progresses in listening comprehension he can be asked to demonstrate his skills in a variety of different ways. There is nothing wrong with combining the skills if the teacher knows what he is asking the student to do. The student who cannot speak cannot demonstrate his proficiency in listening comprehension by speaking. On the other hand, the student who has acquired even minimal speaking skills should be encouraged to use those skills in demonstrating competency in the listening area. He can be taught to summarize orally in the target language what he has heard. Caution must be exercised here. The point is to demonstrate competence in listening comprehension, not in speaking. If the student makes grammatical errors or errors in pronunciation, the teacher may wish to allow him to finish without interruption. The teacher may also wait to note the errors and correct the student later. But the main point is for the student to summarize what he has heard. If he succeeds, he deserves to be praised.

The same means can be used to have the student summarize what he has heard by writing in the target language. It might be better to ask him specific questions and to have him write specific answers. Little by little one can lead him to write a short summary in the target language. He should have developed this skill by level III, and one could then ask him to do the following:

> Listen to a five-minute tape presentation. Then write a summary in Spanish of what you have heard. Be sure to include at least five ideas.
> Evaluation: 80% for content, 20% for mechanics.

One of the most highly skilled competencies is simultaneous translation. We frequently have need of this skill when a person is present who cannot speak English. This particular command of language is most difficult to acquire, for the student who wishes to develop proficiency in simultaneous translation must learn to translate segments of the target language sentences into English without losing the train of thought as it is being phrased by the speaker. If we wish to produce students who have this skill, we must give them opportunity to develop it. In the early stages of language learning, for example, we can play a tape, stop the tape at the end of each utterance, let the student translate the utterance, then let the tape continue. If students begin doing this early, they will regard it as a normal exercise. As the pace increases so will their skill. I would urge, however, that this is a skill for the unusually talented student. If you have a class that is group-paced, you can allow the slower student to listen to a tape and answer questions on it. In another part of the room the gifted student may be listening to the same tape and may be recording his version of it. Care must be exercised as to which students are asked to:

> Listen to a three-minute tape with pauses at the end of each phrase. Translate as many of the segments as you can. There will be twelve phrases.
> Criterion: eight out of twelve correct.

Well-known scholars, such as Albert Valdman (1974) and Simon Belasco (1971), maintain that it is indeed feasible to teach listening comprehension and reading comprehension to large segments of the student population. If we decide to allow students more voice in what they wish to learn, we may find that many prefer the receptive skills. We shall then have to restructure the curriculum to afford them opportunities to hear the language—both in contrived situations and as natives actually speak it. If we examine these skills, if we structure the appropriate activities and utilize the appropriate resources, our students should be able to perform at a much higher level of mastery than most have yet attained.

XII. READING

Reading has always been highly valued as an intellectual skill, because it is through reading that the cultural heritage has been passed on. For people in the New World, cut off, in earlier days, from Europe, reading represented the link to the past and the link to other parts of the present. Books could be imported from Europe and could be enjoyed.

Today, in teaching a foreign language, we have different perspectives on both reading and writing. We have changed the emphasis in writing from the writing of translation passages to free composition, and we have also changed reading from a translation exercise to one recognizably different. Nevertheless, many teachers even now do not understand what their colleagues mean when they speak of the teaching of reading. This area, therefore, more than any of the other skill areas (with the possible exception of composition), can profit from the clarification that the judicious use of performance objectives can supply.

Reading comprises many skills. In the early stages of language learning, and indeed throughout the sequence, students need to be able to vocalize what they see before them in the written target language. They need to put sound to symbol and to read aloud. This act of putting sound to symbol does not require any comprehension at all. In fact, in the first few weeks of language learning the teacher may require the student to vocalize material that he does not understand. This will be particularly true if the language is Spanish, for Spanish is a language with a relatively simple sound system, and a person can learn how to associate the right sounds with the right symbol in a relatively brief period of time. (This would not, however, be true of French which has a more complicated sound system.) While, presumably, the student of Spanish might be able to pronounce individual words in Spanish with some facility, he would still encounter difficulty in putting sentences together, for he would have little knowledge of junctures. A realistic performance objective for the Spanish student after six weeks would therefore be:

> Read aloud a list of twenty isolated words you have not seen previously.
> Pronounce 18 out of 20 correctly.

Students are frequently asked to read what they have previously learned orally. This can be deceptive, for if the student has memorized the phrases, and if the phrases are presented in the same sequence, the student may be *reciting* instead of reading. I suggest that in the early stages of reading the student listen to a tape and follow the text silently. The text should be one that he has not seen previously, although it should contain known vocabulary. The student may listen several times before he is asked to read aloud. He thus acquires the receptive skill of listening before engaging in the productive skill of vocalizing.

Next the student reads the passage aloud. This becomes a performance objective in and of itself. It is quite different from reading aloud a list of isolated words. Both have value, but very different value. When the student reads a passage aloud, he should be sensitive to the cadence and the rhythm. He may still not understand every word, but passively he is acquiring a sense of the passage. The rhythm helps him in this. An appropriate objective might be:

> Listen to a paragraph read aloud (by your teacher or by a voice on a tape).
> Then read the same paragraph aloud.
> Criterion: No more than 5 errors of pronunciation.

Note the wide range of errors. The student is working with a relatively large segment of material. He is still a neophyte. But he is learning that reading aloud is an important skill. Immediately after reading aloud he should be encouraged to read silently for comprehension. He should know what he is saying. He should be given time to ask questions or look up words. He should be told that the task at this point is to get the gist of the passage, not to translate every word. After he has had sufficient time, he should be asked to demonstrate reading comprehension by answering a set of questions. If reading comprehension is the order of the day he should not be asked (during the early stages of level I) to write answers in the target language. He should preferably be given written questions with simple multiple choice answers. He should then be given the correct answers and should be encouraged to correct any errors he has made. He learns from this instant correction. These questions should test the main points in the passage. Most students should get correct answers the first time. If one of the course objectives is to teach the student to read large amounts of material in order to get the gist and the direction, this objective is of prime importance. It is important that students engage in such activities frequently, not just once every four or five weeks. As the student becomes comfortable with the exercise he can be asked to:

> Read the following paragraph, then answer the four questions that follow.
> Check your answers.
> Criterion: Three out of four correct.

Many teachers confuse the teaching of reading comprehension with vocabulary development. It is true that vocabulary development is a vital adjunct of reading comprehension. As the student continues to expand his reading comprehension he absorbs passively words whose meaning he has not yet learned. He also puts cognates into context. He unconsciously accepts words in a passage which he might not identify in isolation. It is at this point that the teacher must keep his performance objectives clearly in front of him. If he wishes the student to develop his vocabulary, he will ask the student to do less reading, to concentrate on designated words, to learn their meaning, to demonstrate that he can identify them in isolation. The judicious use of vocabulary building actually increases reading comprehension. The teacher at this stage might ask the student to:

> Read the paragraph below. Study the twenty words underlined. Then select the most appropriate meaning for each underlined word as it appears in the context of the paragraph.
> Criterion: 15 out of 20 correct.

The definitions may be in English; they certainly would have to be in English in the early stages of language learning, unless meanings were tested by pictures. In the second year and thereafter, meaning could be tested by means of synonyms if the synonyms had been taught previously. As soon as possible the student should work from French to French, Spanish to Spanish, German to German, and (at least in certain methodologies) from Latin to Latin, etc. Nevertheless under certain circumstances it might be more expedient to test the student by means of English equivalents.

The teacher must be aware at this point of asking the student to learn every single word covered in the reading passage. The repetition of the words from one reading passage to another will actually help the student acquire their meanings without having to memorize the meaning of every word. However, if the student commits a few words to memory in each lesson, he will increase his vocabulary at a regular rate and will soon be able to read more efficiently.

In the early weeks of the second year, the student may develop the skill of reading to the extent that he can use this skill to acquire information. At this point the teacher wants to give him performance objectives that center around information which he will use in some new way. An appropriate objective might be:

> Read the two pages attached. Then answer the eight questions that follow. When you come to your conversation group, bring the questions and the answers that you have prepared. You will be asked these questions by a classmate; you will have to state your answers in such a way that your classmates understand you.
> Criterion: 5 out of 8 answers correct.

The criterion for this objective is low, because the student is asked to combine two skills in demonstrating his reading proficiency. The teacher could just as easily ask him to prepare written answers to the questions. In any event, the student is using the skill of reading to acquire information. The information must be used in other forms. Along with the above objective one should find one such as this:

> You will summarize orally five points in the passage that you have just read. If you state any five points, you will have fulfilled the objectives. If you have selected the five most important points, you will receive extra credit.

Now we are asking the student to read and comprehend, to analyze the facts and select the five most important ones, and to state these facts in the target language. He is now moving to the next stage of reading. *In the first stage he learns to read, in the next stage he reads to learn, and in the last stage he organizes what he has learned.* He utilizes the reading passage as a springboard for moving to the next activity which is the beginning of analysis and of summarizing.

If some students have difficulty reaching the above-mentioned objective, you can assign them the following:

> Read the following passage and identify any two ideas or facts found in the passage. Try not to repeat the words of the passage but put the thoughts into your own words.
> Criterion: 2 out of 2 correct.

You may wish to use this objective for the student who has had poor grades. Tell him that if he can do the above objective you will substitute that for some other objective that he was unable to fulfill. In all of our classes there are students who, either through lack of ability, motivation, interest, drive, or because of other problems, are unable to achieve the objectives we assign. We must be flexible enough to substitute other (frequently for them more valid) objectives when students cannot or will not achieve the first ones.

Once the student is able to summarize the passage the teacher may wish to proceed to other areas of reading. I call one of these "reading for accuracy." Here the teacher is interested in the meaning of a specific passage, construction, or word. The best way to emphasize this is to provide a reading passage, underline certain words or expressions, and then ask the student to translate or comment upon the underlined words. One can also give him four different meanings and let him select the correct meaning for the words underlined. The student is working with a small segment of the total picture. He knows that the main point of the passage is to render those particular expressions accurately into English or (at levels III, IV, and V) into a target language paraphrase. Usually this type of performance is required when students have mastered certain idioms and constructions and have seen the passage or a very similar one previously. The purpose behind this type of performance objective is to help the student handle confidently a specific body of material; in this instance he is asked to demonstrate a high level of proficiency in handling a relatively small amount of material.

A sample objective might be:

Read the paragraph below. Translate the underlined words or expressions into English. You will receive two points for each expression, one for the general thought, one for the accuracy of the expression.
Criterion: 18 out of 20 points.

If you assign many of these objectives to the average student you will find that you will need to keep the vocabulary and idiom count very low. The student will slowly build up proficiency if he is able to succeed. You may wish to let him try the same passage twice (but with different questions). It is particularly difficult for language teachers to assume a lower level of proficiency in objectives such as this one. They feel (and perhaps rightly so) that the student should have learned all the expressions. Nevertheless, if they can accept a smaller minimum base of content, the student will be encouraged to keep trying.

Reading is in many ways the most crucial of the skills, for it is a major vehicle to further learning. We should structure the objectives in this area carefully. As we have suggested above, in the early stages the student should read primarily for comprehension. He should also be encouraged to read aloud so that he hears the sounds correctly. He should then be led into reading for accuracy. As soon as possible he should be taught to read for information. Now the teacher can utilize these various skills to build a series of performance objectives that will take the student through four years. It is my contention that during level II he should read primarily for comprehension with less emphasis on accuracy and reading for information. In level III he should read for both accuracy and information. In level IV he should utilize all the skills, and reading should now be second nature to him. He should read to develop vocabulary; he should analyze both for summarizing, for synthesizing, and for style; he should be able to read in depth and should have exposure to *explication de texte;* he should, in the later stages of level IV and in all subsequent courses, utilize his reading skills to aid the development of additional skills.

Content and vocabulary must be developed throughout the four levels as the skills are developed. This is where performance objectives can aid student and teachers. Many teachers are so busy building content coverage that they do not notice whether the student masters either the content or the skill. If they have to write out performance objectives they will quickly see how much they are asking the student to master at each point in his learning. Once more caution should prevail: when you are introducing a new skill or developing a skill that is weak or nonexistent, do not bring in a great amount of content. Concentrate on asking the student to perform the skill. After the student has acquired mastery of the skill it is appropriate to ask him to use the skill with a variety of content and vocabulary combinations. In this way we give him a fair chance to succeed.

If we teach only reading for accuracy the student will not acquire the skills of reading for comprehension. These are quite different. It is most unfair to have the student read for comprehension in class and test him on accuracy, or vice versa. If, like the director of a symphony orchestra, we give each section its turn, we will have a beautifully orchestrated piece of music. In this area performance objectives help us to see what the assignment for each section should be.

Please note that we have not spoken about reading for translating. This is in no way intended as a slur upon the art of translating. It is to say, rather, that reading in foreign language education is primarily for other purposes. Some students early acquire a talent for rendering everything beautifully into their native language. That is not to be discouraged, but it is not to be substituted for the art of reading aloud, reading for comprehension, or reading for accuracy. Nevertheless, the student who is pursuing a scientific career may have much greater need to read for accuracy and the ability to translate than to read broadly for comprehension. This is where a personalization of objectives should take place. It is sad, however, to see large groups of young people who wish to learn to read the language with fluency condemned to do nothing but translation exercises from the target language to English. This in part may be due to the fact that their teachers have never sorted out their students' personal performance objectives in the area of reading.

In the upper levels of language study, and indeed when the student begins to study literature, he needs to pay particular attention to detail, to nuance, to innuendo. He not only needs to comprehend, but he needs to see how writers use words and expressions to convey moods, feelings, and shades of meaning. If he has acquired the appropriate reading skills, he will make a smooth transition to the next level. If, however, he tries to learn literature when he does not have sufficient command of his language skills, he may end up being frustrated, hating literature, and discontinuing his study of language. Literature is for those who have an affinity for words, for those who can use the skill of reading to help them reach the inner chambers of man's thoughts. Until such time as the student acquires these skills, he may be better advised to read more accessible material.

There is, further, one reading objective that may more appropriately be classified under the affective domain, namely reading for pleasure. At some point the student should have acquired enough proficiency in reading to use this skill to bring pleasure to himself. Every teacher desires this to happen, but we are all such perfectionists that we feel that it is necessary to surround the student with only the best—the best in language and the best in literature. Yet how many of us, when we are tired, ourselves pick up a book that may be "beneath us" intellectually! We are reading for pleasure. Good readers frequently read many books that do not improve their minds. They may, on the other hand, happen upon ideas in those very books that help them in their daily lives. Reading for pleasure will help all of us increase our skills in vocabulary, increase our speed, acquire meanings and nuances, and concentrate upon what we are reading instead of how we are reading it. For this reason I believe that every foreign language class should have access to newspapers and magazines, to books, folders, and brochures that provide pleasurable reading. Then the student will see reading as it should be—a means to an end. When he has reached this point, he will not need so much external motivation to continue his study of language. The teacher may encourage students to learn to write their own performance objectives by letting them devise the demonstration portion of the objective:

> Select a book that interests you and read it. Discuss with your teacher an appropriate and enjoyable way of demonstrating your knowledge of the book. Write this up as a performance objective and have your teacher approve it. Then carry out the objective.

The teacher can suggest orally or in writing some acceptable and enjoyable means of demonstrating knowledge: a skit, a debate, a set of cartoons, an essay, a parody, etc. We should always encourage students to devise objectives that differ from those we have suggested.

XIII. LITERATURE

A student's success in literature is closely allied to his success in reading. Students should read literature that is accessible to them. Certain poems and simple short stories may profitably form part of the reading content during the first two levels.

Literature is worth studying because "it is the dream that unites one soul to another" and unless it accomplishes this in some way or another it becomes in the words of Verlaine "littérature," that is, what is cheaply peddled in the name of literature. Literature reveals man to man; it is the verbal document of man's hopes, suffering, and aspirations. It *evokes* these through the medium of language. This is why the classical curriculum assigns the study of literature to the subject that is connected with words, language, be it English or foreign languages, and it is with language that one must begin the study of literature.

In approaching a work of literature the student should know *first* of all *what* it says, what the words mean. *One of the first performance objectives* should ask a student to indicate (via

This chapter is extracted from an article which was first published in *Foreign Language Annals,* Volume 5, Number 3, March 1972. It is reprinted here through the courtesy of the American Council on the Teaching of Foreign Languages.

multiple-choice test, essay, questions and answers, class discussion) that he knows precisely what the author has said. Unfortunately, this is *all* that many teachers of literature do. The student should then be asked *to react to the work in the way that it affects him personally;* for this there is no right or wrong answer, but the student should be taught early to explain his feelings. If his reaction is one of like or dislike, he should say, "I like this because" or "I dislike this because." His opinion is valid in terms of his ability to defend what he feels and to communicate it to others; here he becomes a soul *responding* to another soul. At no point should a student's feelings be held against him, but his rationale can indeed be criticized.

While it can be argued that the student is making a judgment before he has completed all the aspects of learning, at least the judgment is his own. He should learn early to refine previous judgments in the light of later learning. Taste in general reflects personal reactions refined by experiences, habit, and knowledge.

After he has formulated his own opinion the student may be led to consider the work of literature from other points of view, from the point of view of language, of the particular words the author uses to produce various effects which the student felt. He can read the interpretations of others to see further avenues of approach. He can study the literary work by looking at the time and place when the author lived and his preoccupations. He can consider theme, character, and plot development. He can place the work in historical perspective by consulting literary histories, and he can study treatments of the same theme or subject by musicians and artists. The good teacher of literature tries to emphasize several of these points throughout the year, but seldom tells the student in advance that such a highlight will be part of a particular unit. The student may fail to appreciate the emphasis the teacher wishes to make because the teacher has not clearly specified the learning goals.

Students should interpret certain pieces of literature orally. This is particularly true of the drama, the oration, the eulogy. It is not sufficient to read these works silently; they should be declaimed, orated, listened to.

A performance objective that requires a student to give an oral interpretation or reading of a scene of a play, a poem, or an oration will alert the student to the importance of this aspect of literary study. If the teacher wishes to supplement his own talents he should include audio tapes and recordings of dramatic productions as well as full-length movies among his activities. Recordings of dramatic productions can be a helpful aid in the teaching of such literature.

Let me for the moment propose a curriculum in French literature for a four-year high school program. The goals and objectives might be stated as follows. At the end of the first year (level I) the student should be able to:

1. Read aloud a *two-paragraph* (125-150 word) excerpt containing words which he has learned orally; he should make no more than two errors in pronunciation, juncture, or intonation.

2. Answer in English questions in French about the content of a two-paragraph excerpt based on material containing 90% known vocabulary and 10% unknown.

3. Pass a multiple-choice test in French on vocabulary in context; and achieve a grade of 80% to pass. Sample test item: Marie et Suzanne ont une belle *villa.* (a) *voiture* (b) *animal* (c) *vetement* (d) *maison.*

4. Explain in English what a poem is, why it is different from an essay or a short story, what type of language is generally used in poems, why people write poems, why people read poems, the difference between songs and poems (if any).

5. Answer simple factual questions in French about the content of a poem such as Verlaine's "Il pleure dans mon coeur comme il pleut sur la ville."

6. Give four- or five-sentence summaries in French about famous literary personages such as Joan of Arc, Roland, Candide. (Teachers neglect the heroes and heroines of literature, and yet a character such as Roland who is at once admirable, popular, and handsome and who is too proud to blow his horn catches the imagination of today's high school students. Colorful, interesting, and exciting information about these characters can be presented through listening comprehension exercises. If students do not learn, while they are in levels I and II, of the excitement and pleasure that lie ahead of them in the advanced levels, they may never enroll in these.)

Level II objectives would read as follows. At the end of level II the student should be able to:

1. Read aloud one page of a short story containing both known and unknown words; he should make no more than two errors in pronunciation, juncture, or intonation.

2. Read in French and answer in French a series of multiple-choice questions about the material read. This material shall contain

approximately 80% known vocabulary and 20% unknown vocabulary. This area shall test reading comprehension only.

3. Write short summaries in French of what he has read (one- to two-page short stories). He shall first have summarized these stories orally.

4. Explain in English what a short story is, what elements it contains that make it different from an essay or a poem, what type of material is usually covered in a short story.

5. Given 10 vocabulary words from a short story, the student shall use these words in constructing a paragraph that either expresses what happened in the story or his impressions of the story.

6. Give short oral reports in French about one short story writer or one short story which impressed him. He should cite words, incidents, characters, etc., which distinguish the story or writer chosen.

7. Read a novel such as *Le Petit Prince* and be able to do the following:
  (a) Answer in French, using short essay-type answers, factual questions about the plot of the story.
  (b) Discuss in small groups (6-8) in French what happened in the story and the implications of what happened. This would at the start be teacher-dominated but would eventually pass into student hands.
  (c) Pass a multiple-choice vocabulary test on every two chapters (words should be in phrases or sentences). Criterion: 80%.
  (d) Identify significant drawings and quotations by restoring them to proper context.
  (e) Explain in English why this novel can be read at several levels; i.e., why it is a good children's book and why it can be appreciated by adults at all levels of the intellectual hierarchy.
  (f) Relate in French or in English any influences that the author's life had on the writing of the book; this should include point of view, etc.
  (g) Express in French with teacher help the feelings the student has about the ideas, feelings, or attitudes expressed. If this is not possible in French, the student should express his ideas in English and should then be helped to recast them in French.

Level III objectives would ask the student to demonstrate knowledge of the drama and/or the novel. The student would now pass to oral summaries of the plot and content, he would consider the import of the work, he would ask what the physically present symbols indicate, he would begin to analyze and to describe his reactions using a higher level vocabulary, he would write short compositions treating one aspect of the work being studied, his vocabulary development would center around his current reading but would also contain words which he would need for future reading (for example, descriptive terms of nature used for poetry and novel), he would enter the more argumentative phase of discussion, he would continue to lead discussions in French (even at an elementary level).

Level IV objectives would have the student compare and contrast genres, consider in greater depth matters of style, show the role language plays in the development of style, read aloud and perform scenes from a French play, show how the forces of history affected the development of French literature, demonstrate some knowledge of the trends of French literature, and show the effects of the culture upon literature.

I have delineated the first two levels rather carefully because it is there that teachers are hard pressed to begin the study of literature. They pass it off saying that the time is not ripe to begin. Nevertheless, it would seem that if one wants the student to reach the fourth-level objectives sketched above, the groundwork must be laid early. Many teachers do engage in some of the activities expressed but they do not develop them from one sequence to the next because their objectives are not clearly stated—neither their colleagues nor their students nor on occasion they themselves know precisely what they are trying to accomplish. A good example of this is the questioning technique employed in most French classes. The teacher of the fourth-year class is often asking the same types of questions (obviously using new materials) that the second-year teacher asked. At no point has the curriculum indicated that the student should be able to respond using two, three, or more bits of information. Teachers should also vary the strategy of questions and answers, oral summary, quotation taken from the work (and discussed), contrast and comparison with other works read, eliciting student impressions, having one student summarize others' impressions. Yet unless these behaviors are written down and asked of the student, he may repeat the same learning devices year after year.

The study of literature and its enjoyment are, in my opinion, a cumulative effort. Man's greatest creative works are not always accessible to all, but they should, in general, yield great rewards. It is obvious that the works to be studied must be accessible to the student, but they should not necessarily be obvious since only short-lived art yields all it has immediately. The student must be taught where to look for meaning, how to look for nuance, how to compare and contrast the use of language, what makes one type of writing different from another, how the trends that he observes in literature are also present in the other arts, how literature is related to life, to men, and to men's lives, the purposes that literature serves—to embellish, to change, to create and, yes, to destroy.

Most teachers want the student to be able to demonstrate these competencies, but the teacher frequently tries to jam all these skills into one fourth-year course, which acquires a reputation of great difficulty, causing enrollment to dwindle. If this does not occur the teacher does his best, covers what he can, and hopes that someone else will fill in any gaps. If, however, each school stated specific behavioral objectives in the area of literature, if these objectives were distributed appropriately over a four-year period, then students would not be victims of chance—either repeating monotonously each year those skills previously acquired and/or failing to acquire those competencies necessary for further study.

All teachers hope that their students will derive pleasure and profit from the study of their subject. All teachers wish for students to see relevance and value in what they are studying. It is the contention of this writer that such enjoyment, pleasure, and value will best result if the student is given a systematic introduction to the many approaches to literature, to the nuances of language, to the areas of interpretation and the background that his predecessors have found valuable. We do not hold the key to the mystery of where, when, or how the student will find true meaning and pleasure. We should not in the name of enjoyment force our pleasure, our interpretations, our feelings upon him. It is our task to help him discover *his* pleasure, *his* interpretations, *his* feelings; but we can best do this by opening to *him* the avenues of discovery, by making sure that *he* has the skills necessary to *get* him where *he* wishes to go and where *he* is capable of going, by so organizing our curriculum that we do not just put him through a random selection of activities, but that we plan in terms of learning outcomes. Then the student will not be bored, for one activity should lead logically to the next and to a learning outcome; each year's work should not be a dull repetition of what he had the year before but should be the culmination of all he has previously studied. I will grant that the curriculum outlined above may be rather ambitious; it could be modified to meet the needs and objectives of the group, *but it does go somewhere.* I am sure that others could construct better models, could outline different learning outcomes that would be equally valid, but *the important point* is that there *be some outcomes,* that the student and the teacher know at the start, the middle, and the end of the course exactly what is being accomplished. This technique will indeed serve as motivation. We all like to know why we are doing what we are doing, to what extent we are succeeding in it, and what will logically follow. Here is accountability in the best sense, for we are being responsible to our students, to ourselves, and to those who employ us. In so doing we have lost nothing except our vagueness, disorganization, and lack of focus. This seems small loss for so great a gain.

XIV. THE AFFECTIVE DOMAIN and the TEACHING of CULTURE

If many teachers have difficulty associating literature with performance objectives, they may have even greater difficulty associating the affective domain with the teaching of culture. At first glance, therefore, to link the affective domain and the teaching of culture to performance objectives might appear entirely incongruous. What, then, do these two apparently disparate elements have in common, and why should we overcome the difficulty in making that link? They are, first of all, topics that intrigue most language teachers; they are also areas which most teachers feel should be emphasized, and they are areas in which there has frequently been little concrete information to bring into the classroom. However, there is another reason which transcends these: it is that in teaching culture effectively we have the best opportunity to create positive feelings in our students.

The affective domain is the area that emphasizes the learner's feelings, attitudes, and values. Unlike the cognitive domain, which emphasizes *what* a student learns, the affective domain emphasizes the student's *reaction* to what he has learned and is learning. It follows that the first step to be taken in the affective domain belongs to the teacher, since the teacher must orient the student to a new form of behavior that will be expected of him. To some degree the first few weeks of language learning may resemble culture shock. The "traveler" is immersed for a period each day in a new way of life. He is expected to perform in a manner that he has not before experienced. He may be both fascinated and yet put "off base" by this strange new "country."

All learning, however, is built upon an inner enthusiasm that glows and sets the student afire with a desire to know. Learning is a combination of hard work and pleasure. It is folly to expect it always to be pleasurable and often rewarding. Even those areas that most satisfy us require moments and hours of toil, exercise, drill, and rote learning that are not in themselves rewarding. Why, then, do people engage in such tasks without protest? It is because they know why these tasks exist, because they accept the value of such tasks in the total scheme of learning, because they wish to acquire the ultimate rewards that such tasks can offer them, and often because they wish to please a teacher, a parent, or a friend. The main hue and cry of relevancy, I believe, is one of asking how the tasks which teachers assign can possibly have any connection with the learning that the student truly values. Foreign language teachers are often offenders in this area, yet we have good intentions and are frequently unaware of our errors.

In many high schools, if not in most, the student who enters the study of foreign languages has had no previous exposure to the subject. He enters the subject primarily because he believes it will prepare him for college. He may have had encouragement from his mother or father, or from an older sister or brother; it is rare that he has had any first-hand experience with either foreign language learning, a speaker of another language, or a foreign culture. If he comes with any true desire to learn it is because he has become entranced by a different culture, because he wants to travel, because he wants to speak to others and be understood by others. It is seldom because he wishes to conjugate verbs or recite dialogues. Yet while he may wish to learn to speak a foreign language, he does not understand what this learning entails. He probably expects that it will not be easy, but he does not know what will happen to him. He enters with a desire to learn, a sense of anticipation. This anticipation is usually fed for the first day or two as he learns to say, *Guten Morgen* or *Bonjour* or *Buenos días,* but then he is hit with the first dialogue or a conjugation of *-ar* verbs in Spanish. It is in these early stages that many teachers are apparently unaware of the importance of the affective domain, yet it is *here* that the student can be won over to language study. He can be given reasons for doing all the strange tasks that are necessary for learning; he can be taught that the steps he must take are natural steps, although they will seem strange to him; he can be made comfortable while he is learning to perform the strange and exotic. In short, he can be helped over the initial stages of "culture shock" which can overtake him as he begins this new and interesting subject. If some attention is paid to the student's feelings during these early weeks, we may expect him to form lasting, positive attitudes towards language. What specific steps might be taken by the teacher at this time?

During the first days the teacher should explain to the student that imitating sounds is probably unlike anything he has done previously. He should assure the student that there is nothing unmanly or unladylike in uttering strange noises. The learner should be shown that some of the sounds of his native language are also strange, and that he has learned several "difficult" sounds such as the English *R* or *th* or *l.* He should realize that foreigners learning to speak English have to practice for long periods of time those sounds which he makes easily and naturally. It would not be a waste of time to play a tape of foreigners who are speaking English, but who still have trouble with certain sounds. Then the student should be taught to focus on the vowel sounds of the target language and to listen for these. Students have usually not been taught to listen to or to concentrate on particular sounds, and as a rule they do not know how to listen. As a consequence they have difficulty imitating sounds, hence many of them abandon language learning entirely in the earliest stages. It is here that reinforcement, encouragement, and individual help are most needed. No student should be allowed to feel that he is failing during these weeks. The teacher must try to find some aspect of language learning in which the student can succeed. For example, while the student is being given training in pronunciation and imitation in class, he can also be given assignments outside of class dealing with familiar tasks so that he will have some assurance of success. I have found that assignments dealing with people and places both build interests and provide an area where the student can succeed while he is mastering the more difficult initial skills of pronunciation. (We shall consider these in detail in the next chapter.) Thus, the first objective in the affective domain becomes one for the teacher:

All students in my beginning classes during the first three weeks will show signs of success in some aspect of language learning. If I identify one who is having little success with the oral part or the written part of the target language, I will assign him tasks in which he can succeed. No one will be permitted to give up before the end of the fourth week. Criterion: 100% mastery.

A corollary objective for the student would be:

At the end of two weeks the student will fill out a checklist indicating how he *feels* towards various aspects of language study. This attitude survey will in no way be considered part of his grade.

Such a checklist might include items such as the following directions:

Put a check in any column that reflects your feelings; you may check as many as you wish.

This checklist should help the teacher identify what areas he needs to "sell" or explain more fully both to the class and to individual students. (See sample on facing page.)

Since some students learn certain skills more slowly than others, and since the skills required in beginning language classes are skills the student has not previously developed, it is not unrealistic to assume that the teacher may need to individualize instruction during these weeks more than he ever will need to again. He must be able to identify the student who has difficulty memorizing; he must spot the student who has difficulty hearing certain sounds; he must identify the student who cannot imitate what he hears. It is important that the teacher identify the various learning styles by which students operate. For this he may need to break the class into small groups and to assign a specific task to various parts of the class while he works with a small group of students. A second objective for the teacher will be:

At the end of three weeks I will know which of my students have difficulty memorizing, which have difficulty hearing certain sounds, which have difficulty imitating sounds, which are experiencing success, which are spending inordinate amounts of time on the subject, and which need to be challenged more.
Criterion: 100% accuracy.

	think it's fun	think it's silly	like to do it	don't like to do it	would like help in learning how to do it	know how to do it	don't know how to do it
Pronunciation Exercises							
Imitating Sounds							
Learning Dialogues							
Watching Films							
Conversing in Spanish							
Memorizing Vocabulary							
Writing Homework							
Doing Restaurant Assignment							
Learning about Cubans							

A student performance objective which mirrors this:

> At the end of three weeks each student will write a short paragraph (or one to three paragraphs) describing how he practices pronunciation, memorizes dialogues, learns vocabulary. He will include any reactions he has to the learning, such as "It takes too much time" or "I wish we had more work in this area" or "This is hard for me."

I call this type of performance objective a confluent objective (see Brown, 1971) since the student reveals to the teacher both his own strategy of learning and his feelings about his learning.

In order to accomplish this objective the teacher will need to meet with small groups of students. If a language lab or a tape recorder and earphones are available two-thirds of the class can work on listening comprehension, dialogues, or imitation of sounds. The teacher can also use written assignments or reading assignments that deal with study skills as a means of occupying some students while he works with others.

There is a close connection between the cognitive domain and the affective domain. It is difficult to appreciate that which we do not know. It is hard to understand a people or an idea about which we have only misconceptions. Many students entering a foreign language class know little or nothing about the people whose language they are studying. They may have certain stereotyped ideas, but frequently these are fallacious. I consider it absolutely essential that they acquire some information about the target people and culture during the early weeks of language learning. They can best do this by seeing films, listening to tapes, and listening to the teacher. In order to get the time for small groups the teacher can record on a tape a short *causerie* or chat about the people and the country; he can then select slides from his own collection or that of a colleague and set up a synchronized slide-tape presentation. This technique will be considered in greater detail in Chapter XV.

One of the reasons students see little value in studying a foreign language is that they see no connection between it and the other subjects they are studying. In the early stages the teacher can profitably help the student to an understanding of what language actually is, how language is used, what the value of language is. We teachers often take this for granted, but the student has had little exposure to such thinking. If he sees how his foreign language study may parallel that of other areas such as speech correction, drama, music, reading, composition, he may sense in language study more than the meanderings of deranged minds. It is at this point that the teacher can explain to him the reason for learning dialogues, that there are patterns in English as well as in the target language. He can ask the student to list the first ten sentences he would teach a foreigner to say in English; he can ask the student to conjugate in English certain verb forms to show all that is necessary to know about them in language learning. These moments of helping the student to understand the nature of language will pay great rewards if the student does not engage in fighting the learning process. An appropriate student performance objective might be:

> List five of the components of language. Which skills of English do you consider that you possess to the highest level? Listening? Speaking? Reading? Writing? Give at least one reason for:
>
> (a) memorizing dialogues;
> (b) doing structure drills;
> (c) writing substitution exercises;
> (d) reading aloud in a foreign language.

If the student is unable to supply answers for the above, the teacher can assume that the student does not understand *why* he is performing certain tasks. It is, of course, possible that the student will list reasons which the teacher accepts, but which he, the student, does not! Nevertheless the student will show that he can state *some* reason for doing the assigned tasks.

Learning a language is work. But there are ways of making work pleasant. Pronunciation is a detailed task, not an easy one. Singing helps many students to pronounce. Certain types of songs emphasize difficult sounds. Students like to sing (at least some of them do). If singing forms part of the day's activity it will become a routine part of class. We should encourage those who perform well to put on a short program for the others and for other classes. Many apathetic language students have been rescued by music.

It is always rewarding to show that you have learned a great deal in a short time. In the junior high and high school many students are "turned on" as performers, and parents make a most supportive audience when *their children* are on stage. Both students and parents would profit from performances given relatively early in the school year, such as Thanksgiving time. Neophyte language students can be involved in group singing and in individual performances of short songs in the target language. These activities are a form of expression, and once again individual differences must be recognized. There must always be a place for the student who does not wish to perform publicly.

It is ironic, therefore, that while language teachers bemoan the fact that students find their subject irrelevant, they fail to implement the one aspect of language learning that could make the subject relevant to both the learner and the evaluator of the course, namely, the culture. Presenting culture is not an act of which a teacher should be ashamed. Nor should a teacher be apologetic because he does not feel competent to teach every aspect of the culture. This concession in no way denies that teaching of culture needs to be structured. It should not be a haphazard activity that occurs only on Friday afternoons, nor should it be a substitute for good, thorough language teaching. It should be the handmaiden, the accompaniment and an integral part of a sound language program. In the early stages it should be the motivational force that helps the student through the early and sometimes difficult entrance skills. As the course progresses it should be the content and the meat of the first level since it represents what most students really want to know about the target people. It should be sequenced and developed as the language learning curriculum is developed, so that the student does not repeat at each level the cultural objectives and activities of the previous level. Language teachers should establish solid, realistic performance objectives in the area of culture. They should formulate activities based on resources that are made available to the student. The cultural objectives should be evaluated and graded just as the language objectives are evaluated and graded. At the end of a four- or five-year sequence in language study the student should have a knowledge of the people and the culture as well as of the language.

Language is communication between people or peoples. If one of the communicators has little or no desire to communicate with others, he will not expend the necessary energy to learn to communicate. Culture, then, is the means of motivating him to wish to communicate. In the broad sense culture is everything that one learns about a foreign language speaker, his country, and his habits. It is the past that makes him the way he is today; it is the present—his problems, his traditions, his goals, his point of view—that makes him behave as he does; it is the future—his orientation, where he is directed, what he dreams of—that will help us to deal with him with a measure of understanding.

But, as stated earlier, attitudes trigger action for most of us. Our attitudes in large measure determine how we use our time. Language must be associated with the learner's short-range and long-range goals. We as teachers may feel that language is important for its humanistic values, but if the student is looking for pragmatic reasons for studying something, then we must give him those reasons if they honestly exist. *It is not necessary that the student study languages for the same reasons that we studied them.* It is more important that we accept the student where he is and build on the tolerance that he has for language study. He may in the course of time become persuaded that our reasons are more valid than his. But if we alienate him in the early stages of language study, if we try to impose our reasons on him, if we insist that our point of view is the only valid point of view, he will not stay around long enough to be persuaded.

Students must be allowed to discuss their points of view with honesty. A wholesome professionalism must be the order of the day. A teacher does not need to be persuaded of a student's point of view any more than a student needs to be persuaded of a teacher's point of view. Both need to be exposed to the other—and to listen. Objectives that cause students to state a point of view and support that point of view *can* contribute to positive student attitudes. Such an objective might be:

> State four reasons why in your opinion Miami has become a principal residential city for Cuban refugees. You may support your opinions with articles from newspapers, magazines, etc.

Some of us see value in a subject which does not have immediate importance for us. We may elect to continue it, but only at a later date. If our attitudes have been positive, if we have enjoyed the experience of studying the subject, if we continue to see value in it, then we will continue this study at an early opportunity. If learning is a life-long process we must accept the development of a positive attitude toward learning as a most important objective. Teachers need to bear in mind that their most important performance objective may be:

My students will see enough value in language study that 90% of them will enroll in the next level of language learning during the next two years.

Students need to develop a point of view about the subject, but that point of view is always subject to change. We are often influenced after the fact, and while we are fighting hardest to reject a point of view we may actually be on the threshold of accepting it. If the individual with whom we are arguing leaves us room to grow and time to develop we may all change our minds. As students honestly examine their points of view, they may discover certain discrepancies, some disparities, some errors. They may then change because they are convinced that the change is good. If they value the teacher, they will seek, but not always immediately accept, the teacher's point of view. The teacher who honestly *shares* his thoughts will find much greater acceptance and influence than the teacher who *imposes* them. Teachers, therefore, may appropriately set the following objective for themselves:

My students will formulate a point of view on the reasons for studying a foreign language. This point of view will reflect their interests, needs, goals, and abilities. Whether the point of view is positive or negative, the student will supply supporting evidence for his views.
Criterion: 95% positive by end of the year.

Notice that this is a *teacher* objective. The teacher wishes to change attitudes. He wishes the student to change his point of view, but he wishes him to do it honestly. The teacher may not always reach this objective, just as some students may not always reach their objectives, but the teacher will be aware of his successes and his failures. He will deal with attitudes honestly and openly.

Most teachers recognize that there is value in extracurricular activities, but many feel that they have limited importance. However, it is precisely these activities that students often remember long after they have forgotten the verbs and the dialogues learned in class. The extracurricular activities were pleasurable and had some meaning. Perhaps, as with singing, they gave the student the rare opportunity of showing off a skill which he had learned. They may have provided him with a new experience, or have taken him out of the drudgery of the classroom. They may even have provided a change of pace. Perhaps they provided insights into why he was doing what he was doing. Teachers like extracurricular activities because the students give of their own time, and teachers recognize the value of this investment. They frequently do not recognize that the student may need directed exposure in class before he will invest his own time in an activity. A teacher performance objective might be:

> I will assemble a series of objectives from which the student will be asked to select one or two. Each of these objectives will be designed to involve him in one of the following: reading magazines in the target language, attending foreign films, becoming acquainted with foreign students, preparing and eating foreign foods, traveling to foreign countries.
>
> Criterion: 80% of my students will continue with one of these activities after the objective has been met.

Teachers in many subject areas are making affective education a part of the daily routine and a part of the standard curriculum. Values clarification is very popular, and certain of the techniques used by writers such as Sid Simon and Howard Kirschenbaum (1972), Howard Bessell and Uvaldo Palomares (n.d.) work very well in the foreign language classroom. We have already mentioned "voting." Another similar topic is ranking. Students in second-year classes can be asked to rate in order of importance such topics as pollution, corruption in government, and abortion. All this is done in the target language. There is no right or wrong answer to these questions, but while we are working on one aspect or skill such as listening comprehension, we can be raising questions of real concern to students.

Two writers in the foreign language field, Virginia Wilson and Beverly Wattenmaker have applied these principles to the foreign language classroom (1973). They offer exercises appropriate in beginning as well as in advanced classes to help students express their feelings. Both have found success in their own classes—not only with helping students develop more positive attitudes towards learning, but also in helping them to communicate more effectively in the foreign language.

As more writers and teachers devote greater attention to the affective domain, we will evolve more techniques for helping students express feelings. One author, George Isaac Brown, has pleaded for confluent education—"an integration or flowing together of the *affective* and *cognitive* elements in individual or group learning—sometimes called humanistic or psychological learning" (Brown, 1971, p.3). Brown and his colleagues are concerned that students develop feelings about their surroundings, their classmates and themselves.

There is no reason why self-awareness cannot be included in the content area. Teenagers are quite naturally interested in themselves, and "finding oneself" has become the order of the day. We need more course objectives in the speaking area which raise questions such as: What do you want to be? Where do you want to live? What do you think ought to be done in the classroom . . . the school . . . the community . . . the country? What are your interests? State one positive fact about yourself. Suggest an adjective that describes you. Students at all levels can handle certain of these questions. Self-discovery need not always be an accident of fate.

Personalization implies the recognition and acceptance of the unique qualities of each human being. Programs whose objectives are built upon student interest in the content area will probably produce better skills development. As the foreign language teacher becomes more aware of the interests, abilities, and needs of his students he will write better cognitive and affective objectives. He will guide his students to an expression of their own reactions and feelings from simple mundane matters to expressions of literary perceptions. If we win the battle of attitude, there will indeed be more competent language learners at all levels.

Can we measure performance in the affective domain? Yes, indeed we can. Should we measure performance in the affective domain? Yes, I think we should. Should we *grade* performance in the affective domain? No, I do not believe that this should form part of the grade or recorded evaluation in a foreign language course. We each have a right to our attitudes. No person, even a teacher, has the right to control another's mind. It is also difficult to determine when we have controlled another's point of view. If our job depends on our keeping quiet when a critical issue is discussed, many of us will keep quiet. Students react in the same way. If their grade depends on teacher approval, they will quickly learn to give the answer that is desired. As soon as the threat is over, however, and as soon as they are removed from the classroom, they like to demonstrate their independence by reacting in the opposite direction. Few students object to being graded on what they know; most resent being graded on what they think or feel. Many of them enjoy being able to interpret or use information on tests in new and creative ways, if they are assured that the point of view expressed will not be held against them. Only if students respond honestly to a teacher can the teacher determine whether or not he has altered their attitudes during the year. How can one measure this? By interviews, by questionnaires, by surveys.

As students learn that teachers use the information gleaned from these interviews and surveys to give them immediate help and to improve the course for their successors in later years, they will become more honest and open with the teacher. They may come to recognize that some of their frustrations are an inherent part of learning. If they finish each year of language learning on a positive note, they will be more inclined to return to language study, some time, some place.

I must end this chapter with the following statement: Most students acquire positive feelings towards subjects when they have accomplished tasks and have achieved a measure of success. *Trying to keep students happy by demanding little of them does not lead to positive feelings in the long run.* The students may even feel cheated. Probably almost every college adviser of undergraduates has heard the following complaint: "Oh, yes, I got A's in the subject, but I can't take any more of it now! The teacher was too easy on us! We didn't have to learn anything!" There is no denying that good grades create better attitudes than poor grades, but most students value basic honesty. They want to be challenged, but not overwhelmed; they want to learn, but not be overworked; they want to be heard, but not be abandoned; they want to be amused, but not played with. Thus, the essential objective for the language teacher must be:

> My students will acquire the necessary skill, knowledge, and attitudes to enter and complete successfully the next level of language learning.

We then must leave the student to work out his own destiny.

XV. THE COGNITIVE DOMAIN
and the TEACHING
of CULTURE

In the last chapter we examined the areas of attitudes and feelings. We found that most students enter foreign language study with a desire to know more about the people and the country where the language is spoken. If this is true, and certain questionnaires and surveys appear to substantiate it (Nostrand, 1974, pp. 266-67), then it follows that student attitudes will be kept at a positive level if students continue to learn about the people and their culture.

Attitudes often are based on what we know or think we know. It is at times difficult to differentiate between the point where the affective domain ends and the cognitive domain begins. Our opinions of people frequently reflect what we *know* about them. So it is with culture. The amount and kind of information we teach students about the people and the country determine to some degree the attitudes they hold toward those people.

During the past decade foreign language educators have turned their attention increasingly to the teaching of culture, and the numerous workshops, publications and speeches dealing with the topic reflect the general interest of the profession. Nevertheless, there has not yet emerged a curricular structure for the teaching of culture. Most writers or speakers deal with one or more aspects of culture, but few have devoted attention to structuring a curriculum—two-year or four-year in sequence—with sequential objectives or even units of culture. This lack is also reflected in textbooks. While most textbook authors agree that it is necessary to deal with culture, they include only smatterings of it to make the book attractive. There is a good reason for this: the profession is not in agreement concerning a format for the teaching of culture. Some members of the profession are, however, turning their attention to the topic.

In my opinion cognitive objectives in the area of culture need structuring. This is not to deny the overwhelming task that this entails. H. Ned Seelye, in a speech to the Minnesota Association of Foreign Language Teachers in October, 1972, used the term "vulture culture"; under this title culture is seen as a huge tapestry spread out for teachers, and the individual teacher, like a vulture, soars in the sky above it and swoops down to pick up a thread of the culture. He then examines the thread, raises questions such as why this aspect of culture exists and what function it serves, and then restores the thread to the tapestry.

I agree with Ned Seelye that we should not examine a single element of culture in isolation, contrast or compare it to one of the student's own culture, and then abandon it. We have an obligation to show how that aspect of culture fits into the entire tapestry. Howard Nostrand has given in-depth treatment of the topic in his chapter, "Empathy for a Second Culture" (1974). He suggests selection of items be based on student interest and also on the nature of the phenomenon to be grasped (pp. 319-20). Nostrand continues, "A sociocultural system, and any of its variant lifestyles, is a whole whose parts color one another. This is why a value, a custom, or a word has no one-to-one counterpart in another culture" (p. 273). Nostrand then develops the idea that the efficient use of the student's cognitive capacity, and that of the teacher as well, requires the organization of what we know about the sociocultural whole into some structure. How, then, do we reconcile the idea of student-centered learning—starting where the student is—and the structuring of the sociocultural whole? Nostrand suggests that the best means is a structured inventory, designed with a "handle"—the main themes of the culture being studied. He further refines the definition of a theme in this context as one of the pervading concerns that make up a culture's value system (p. 277) and suggests that there would never be more than a dozen or so such themes. If we have identified the themes, we may then start from the student's objectives and place what he wants to know in the context of relationships that will make the true nature of the culture understandable (p. 280).

How can this model help us in the writing of performance objectives in the area of culture? We have to look at the age, maturity, and interests of the students for whom we are constructing course purposes and course objectives.

Cognitive cultural objectives should reflect course purposes. It is reasonable to expect that beginning students at the high school level should have different cultural objectives from beginning students at the fifth-grade level or beginning students at the college level.

Nostrand divides his "emergent model" into four subsystems which he adapted from the sociologist Talcott Parsons. These subsystems are: the *cultural subsystem,* which is made up of the culture's dominant values, habits of thought, and assumptions, plus its empirical knowledge, art forms, language, paralanguage, and kinesics; the *social subsystem,* which comprises interpersonal and group relations, shaped by institutions whose component roles are governed by norms; an *ecological system,* which describes the population relationships with its subhuman environment, and an *individual subsystem,* which describes what a given person does with the shared patterns—conforming, rebelling, exploiting, or innovating.

Our task is to select from the subsystems and ultimately from the themes those areas which best meet our students' needs *at the time we are teaching them.* We will, in the long run, need some measure of agreement with our colleagues so that the themes we are undertaking are not repeated in the same manner year after year while other themes are given no consideration.

Harry Reinert showed that in 1968 students in the Edmonds School District near Seattle rated learning about the foreign culture as the most important substantive value of foreign language study (Reinert, 1970). This would lead teachers to conclude that cultural objectives should form a part of language study from the beginning of the course. What type of cognitive objectives might then be implemented? During these early stages the student needs additional reasons for going through the steps necessary to learn the language. If he discovers that many people living in his own city speak the language he is learning, he may develop greater motivation to learn. If he sees slides or films about the country, he may acquire a greater desire to do the necessary work. A student performance objective could be:

> Answer 20 multiple-choice questions about Spanish-speaking people living in *Chicago* (city) or *Illinois* (state). Material covered in this test will be found on tapes and in the books and articles on the attached list.

This information would derive from the themes that are reflected in the course purposes. The teacher is not splattering bits of information that may or may not be gathered together later. He is rather selecting those components that are most appropriately used in the beginning of the course, and he now has a framework in which to work.

Nostrand (1974) also makes some appropriate suggestions for the proper scope of the culture area to be studied. He suggests that we equate the culture area with the language area, but that we select one sociopolitical subarea (such as one country within the Hispanic area) and one socioeconomic class, choosing subareas and classes with which the learner can begin to feel at home. He states that the initital focus could be even more narrow for some sociocultural patterns—a single city for observing municipal government, a single age group for leisure activities. He continues the discussion by urging that the range of sympathies and comprehension be broadened from the point of entry to other countries or regions, to other social classes, to other ages, other ethnic and religious groups, much as one broadens his range of interests in studying the history and culture of his own country.

How does a teacher begin to write cognitive objectives in this area? He begins by reflecting the course purposes, and he refines these purposes by using an outline such as the following:

LEVEL I	*SKILLS*
Mexico—content	
Family Customs	Identification
Famous Singers	Identification
Classes in the Society	Classification and Identification

LEVEL II
Mexico, Cuba, Puerto Rico

Leisure Time Activities	Explanation and Summarization—Pen Pals
Family Customs	Explanation of Cultural Pattern
Famous Artists	Identification
Types of Music	Imitation and Application
Problems of Spanish- Speaking Peoples Living in the United States	Observation, Presentation, and Analysis

LEVEL III
South America

History and Origins	Identification and Analysis
Famous Monuments	Identification
Classes in Society	Analysis and Synthesis
Revolutions—How They Are Born and Bred	Analysis, Synthesis, and Evaluation
Governments	Analysis and Synthesis

LEVEL IV
Spain

Current Philosophies	Identification, Analysis, Synthesis
Great Men of Letters	Identification
Implications of Words as *Hermano*	Analysis, Synthesis, and Evaluation

While this outline may seem to reflect a hodgepodge, it actually represents an introduction to the study of culture. In four years one cannot expect students to become proficient in all aspects of the culture of the Spanish-speaking world. The teacher could tighten the cultural tapestry by comparison and contrast techniques, by asking in the second year how the cultural patterns of Cubans, Mexicans, and Puerto Ricans resemble each other and how they differ. He could connect the student's study of the classes in society the first year with his study of leisure time activities in the second year. Thus, before writing objectives, the first step is to produce an outline of the components to be studied and the skills that will be required. Then one should build bridges from one aspect of the culture to the next.

Many language teachers are troubled when they teach culture, for they feel it wrong to take the needed time away from language instruction. However, teaching about the target culture does not have to remain in English. It is seldom too early to bring in short tapes of broadcasts—two or three sentences of a weather report that was taped from a broadcast. These sentences can be played several times after the student has had the lesson on weather. Here the student is making a contact with the real language, the language as it is spoken by others, and he usually responds to this type of stimulus. The student can then be asked to do the following:

Listen to the taped weather broadcast; then answer the six (6) multiple-choice questions in Spanish that follow. After that, summarize any similarities or differences that you notice between these broadcasts and those that you normally hear on the radio or see on the television on your own local stations.

Exchange students and native speakers who live in the area or in surrounding areas bring an excitement to the classroom, and if such persons speak in short, slow sentences even beginning students may understand them. Let the students at the end of one semester of language study ask the native some questions. Help them prepare questions and practice them so that they will not be too shy. Encourage them to formulate questions that elicit information. This information can be based on the themes and components of themes being studied.

If there are no natives in the area encourage the students to acquire pen pals. Most of the AAT's have services for providing pen pals for students. Pen pals provide motivation at an early date, and when the student has learned how to write in the target language, they provide motivation in that skill as well. One performance objective could be:

You will make contact with some native either in person or by mail. You will formulate in class a series of five or more questions which you will ask the native either orally or in writing. You will then write up your answers and will share them with the class.

Attitudes and feelings cannot be determined by others. They can, however, be changed frequently if the person acquires further information, if he comes to know an individual or a group better. By putting the student into direct contact with a person from a different country the teacher sets the stage for the change to a more positive attitude. We tend to fear and mistrust those whom we do not know. We identify with those who are compatible, non-threatening, with those who reinforce us either by being similar to us or by finding us exciting and challenging.

If one of the purposes of studying a foreign language is for the student to understand peoples of different cultures, then we must help the student to understand the feelings of those people who live near him. At the present time these feelings are not always positive (at least in the student's mind). If we assign objectives that require the student to assemble information, examine that information, and draw conclusions, we may help him find the road to understanding. For example:

> Examine the statement that follows. Then consult five different resources (people, books, newspapers, magazines, etc.) Using these resources write an explanation of the statement and document your findings by citing the resources:

> In Spanish-speaking neighborhoods of Chicago, New York, and San Francisco (as well as in many other cities) the people insist that all personnel who work in second-language teaching, neighborhood houses, and welfare agencies be native Spanish speakers.

This type of objective requires the student to research a topic and examine what others have to say. He is not asked to accept or reject any of the statements. Such objectives, done in the target language, provide meaningful course content at the upper levels.

In teaching culture in the cognitive area we must begin where the student is. We must help him to an understanding and appreciation of those speakers of the target language who live nearest to him. We can no longer neglect the culture of French-speaking Canada, and we must address ourselves to Spanish-speaking peoples within the United States.

If the student becomes interested in "culture with a small 'c'," he may well go on to a study of "Culture with a capital 'C'." The profession has responded well to a plea for more material in the area of culture. Nostrand's bibliography (1974) gives many references in this area. Publications such as *Accent on ACTFL* abound in interesting cultural activities. It is important, however, for teachers to state what they expect students to learn from an experience and what they expect them to be able to do as a result of the experience.

One also should not neglect role-playing in the teaching of culture. J. Lawrence McWilliams, Foreign Language Supervisor of the

Jefferson County Public Schools in Colorado, and his teachers conduct superlative language camps on various weekends. Students are required to pass through customs, fill out documents, endure the inspection of suitcases, etc. It should be easy to write a performance objective for such activities:

> You will describe orally the steps involved in passing through customs. State the preparations that you need to make in advance. Explain why, in your opinion, Europeans have so many customs formalities. Do any of these formalities exist for travelers coming to the United States? For American travelers returning from Europe?

Culture, like language, needs to be experienced. Nostrand makes the point that we need both experiential techniques and cognitive techniques for students. However, learning is often reinforced by summarizing and reviewing. Students need to feel a sense of accomplishment. Jacqueline Elliot recounted at the 1973 meeting of the Tennessee Foreign Language Association (Nashville, Tennessee) how students in French had enjoyed learning to "count off" in French. Instead of "Eeny, Meany, Miney, Moe" one says "Une oie, (one goose), deux oies, trois oies, quatre oies, cinq oies, six oies, sept oies!" The French teacher quickly sees the connection with "C'est toi" ("It's you" or "You're it"). Professor Elliot urged the group to summarize the learning by stating "See what you learned today." I would consider the following an excellent cultural and linguistic performance objective:

> Count off in French (within a group) until no one is left. Then explain how the French system of counting off differs from the American system.

H. Ned Seelye (1970, pp. 569-71) provides some interesting examples of performance objectives that can be used for teaching cultural concepts. He suggests (as a purpose) that students come to the realization that cultural patterns exist because they work. One performance objective that Seelye lists to implement this purpose is:

> Anticipate the effect which changing one variable has on other cultural components, where the major variables are a railway strike, a student demonstration, an impending *golpe de estado,* and the cost of stability in terms of populace unrest—or any other set of variables which meets the teacher's approval and is announced well in advance of the simulation—by either participating as a player in three simulates of at least three hours' duration each, or by being on the winning team of a simulate. (p. 570).

Seelye offers the following commentary on the objective:

> Since the purpose of this performance objective is to *illustrate* the stated purpose, the specific components of the illustration (railway strike, etc.) are strictly arbitrary. While ideally the student would choose his own examples, some students need the security which comes from having all of the components of an assignment spelled out for them. The technique most suited to teaching a student an understanding of a complex system is simulation. Unfortunately, the FL profession has yet to design appropriate simulates. Meanwhile, perhaps the teacher can interest a few bright students in working up an unsophisticated game involving role playing. (p. 570)

As I stated above, in no way should culture be disassociated from language. It is true that during the beginning stages, the student will not be able to cope with culture in the target language. Howard Nostrand and others have advocated homework assignments (in English) dealing with cultural topics while the student is in the process of acquiring the basic linguistic skills. However, students can be taught to associate appropriate cultural images with the vocabulary being studied. *Pain* and *café* evoke certain images to a Frenchman that differ from the American's image of "bread" and "coffee." Seelye provides an objective of this type:

> Identify with eighty percent accuracy, from several pictures of the same type of object, the one which most commonly represents the following in Spanish-speaking countries: abrigo, abuelo, adulto, aeropuerto, almacén, almuerzo, alumno, Argentina, autobús, (etc.). (p. 572)

The student is not only learning a vocabulary word (indeed, he may well have learned it earlier), but he is associating the word with its cultural image.

John L. D. Clark (1972, p. 247) states that a basic problem to the teaching and testing of culture is that of defining the specific cultural patterns to be taught and tested. Examining Committees of groups like the Educational Testing Service have encountered this difficulty. Until there is at least as much consensus on this topic as there is on the teaching of literature, each school will have to construct its own set of cultural objectives.

Nevertheless, with the plethora of activities in the area of culture, with the popularity of learning packets, with the attention being paid to the topic both from the podium and in the professional publications, teachers should have a wealth of material from which to draw.

Performance objectives can well serve the teaching of culture because they point up the need for outcome—what can the student do after the experience? How does he feel about the experience? They also emphasize the need for a framework, a structure, an organization to the teaching of culture. The inherent danger is that the learner will have only fragmentary views of the culture. A judicious use of performance objectives can eliminate this danger, especially if those objectives are carefully screened.

XVI. SCREENING PERFORMANCE OBJECTIVES

Students enjoy variety and structure in a curriculum. They want to feel that they have attained a measure of success. An effective curriculum design depends on an adequate and appropriate mixture of good performance objectives. It is possible for a school to have written a series of very fine performance objectives, each one explicitly stating what student performance is expected, and it is possible that each objective in itself may be well thought out and well planned, but still the *set of objectives* may be inappropriate, unrealistic, or too removed from reality to be effective. The purpose of this chapter is to offer some suggestions for reviewing the set of objectives so that the curriculum as a whole will be functional and appealing.

The critics of performance objectives usually center their arguments around the impact of the total foreign language curriculum upon students, and there is no denying validity to their arguments. They frequently set forth the following objections:

1. the foreign language curriculum is only a paper and pencil curriculum; insufficient attention is paid to the development of oral skills;

2. there are too many low-level cognitive objectives in the total foreign language curriculum;

3. the totality of the curriculum design does not yield the results desired, that is, the students do not have the desired behaviors at the end of the course;

4. all students are asked to meet the same objectives;

5. student performance is specified in advance, and students are programmed like robots into the "objective machine" which turns them all out with the same trivial competencies.

The materials which were developed by C. L. Jenks and associates at the Far West Laboratory (Jenks, 1972) and which were used at the 1971 ACTFL Performance Objective Symposium (Chicago, Illinois) utilized a procedure that should help teachers, department chairmen, and curriculum directors select an appropriate mixture of objectives. Some of these ideas for screening objectives are set forth above in the discussion of the goal refinement system in Chapter III. These same principles are relevant to the discussion at hand:

1. First, develop a set of purposes that is in harmony with the school philosophy. If there is no philosophical basis for the writing of objectives, the curriculum may wander all over the spectrum. If, however, the school has a philosophical basis for all its programs, the language program should be in harmony with this philosophy.

2. Next, screen each individual objective to make sure that it meets the criteria of guidance, relevance, and feasibility.

3. Then review the set of objectives to determine whether or not it contains an appropriate representation of cognitive and affective behaviors, whether or not it is broad enough to cover the subject adequately, and whether or not all objectives are internally consistent.

The writers of the Far West Laboratory materials feel that a complete set of performance objectives should contain an adequate sampling of the most important learning outcomes and that the set, taken as a whole, should contribute to the attainment of the goals and subgoals.

It is to the process of screening that we turn our attention in this chapter. One educator, E. J. Duffy, has stated that the innovations of the 1960's revealed the weaknesses that have always existed in curriculum design—weaknesses particularly evident in any curriculum that has been converted or translated into performance terms (Duffy, 1974). Many departmental curricula have in fact had no philosophic basis, depending for their effectiveness almost entirely on the intelligence and personality of the individuals who happened to be teaching. In many instances they have also depended to a large extent on the textbook or set of materials that had been selected, for teachers frequently even now engage in little decision-making except to select a textbook which they then either embrace wholeheartedly or modify by addition or deletion. They may select activities to accompany the textbooks, and they often use tests created by the authors of the textbook materials.

I should like at this point, however, to offer some practical suggestions for those teachers who are trying to decide what type of curriculum they should establish for students, hence which objectives should play a major role in the curriculum. Note that in many instances one decision triggers several others.

Consider the following questions:

1. Will there be

a. one foreign language curriculum for all students?
(if answer is a., continue in this column.)

b. two or more options open to students studying foreign language?
(If answer is b., continue in this column.)

2. Will this curriculum be designed for the college-bound student?

2. Will the options be based on rate of learning, content, skills, student needs, student abilities, or student interests?

3. Are most students who are enrolled in foreign languages college bound? Do they have similar goals?

3. Will there be "tracks" or ability grouping?

4. Is the prime goal or purpose for students to speak the foreign language?

4. Will instruction be individualized or will different classes be established?

5. Is there to be an equal emphasis on all four skills?

5. For what types of students are you designing your curricula?

6. Will all students be graded similarly?

6. Are you designing the options in order to increase or maintain enrollment? If so, have you surveyed the students to determine their interests?

7. Will all students be expected to meet the objectives within the same period of time?

8. Does reading have a higher priority than writing?

9. Will all students be expected to meet the same objectives? to engage in the same activities? at the same time?

10. Do you have any problems in enrollment? If so, list your problem areas.

11. Have you received input about the type of student and the type of curriculum that parents and counselors feel necessary?

7. Will you use the same grading procedure in all areas of option?

8. Will these options operate on a schoolwide basis or only in foreign languages?

Note that the question in column *a* should help you clarify the type of students for whom you are designing a single curriculum. They are also useful in helping you determine the type of curriculum that can best meet your needs. If you have ideas of a single curriculum for the college-bound student, and if your enrollment is dwindling, this is a fact you should face before screening your objectives. You may decide that the only type of curriculum that is feasible for your school is one designed for the college bound, but that you must make it quite relevant for all students or you will continue to lose many. In designing a single curriculum teachers must remember that it is hard to be all things to all people. Decision-making can be very painful at times.

If you choose column *b,* your task is easier but more voluminous. You need to design a separate set of performance objectives for each option. In some instances you may use similar objectives and vary the content or the mastery level. This sort of change, though small, does make the objectives different. If you are designing different options you must know clearly the type of student for whom each option is intended. Screen each set of objectives as carefully as possible so that you truly reflect the differences you are seeking to establish. All the questions contribute to the quantity and the quality of the objectives you are now screening and selecting.

As you begin the screening process I would suggest that you look at the adequacy of the subject matter coverage. The greater temptation is to include any objective that anyone on the team thinks important. This minimizes conflict at the time, but it may result in an unrealistic set of objectives that cannot be attained. It is better to agree on some number of objectives even if that number is modified as the team progresses. Then the team will evaluate the objectives within a known framework. It is easier to write objectives in the area of grammar, vocabulary, reading, and writing than it is to write objectives in the areas of conversation, listening comprehension, and culture. This can lead to a very unbalanced curriculum unless teachers exercise due care in the screening. As you screen objectives ask the following questions:

1. Do I have a suitable number of objectives that require the student to demonstrate true conversational skills, not just repetition or memorization of material?

2. Do I have a suitable number of objectives in the area of listening comprehension? Are these objectives varied? sequential?

3. Do I have a suitable number of objectives dealing with culture? Do I have a selection that can be implemented at all times during the school year?

4. Do I have a number of objectives that deal with requisite study skills needed to help the student succeed in foreign language learning? Do I have some objectives that help the student learn how to learn a foreign language?

5. Do I have a number of objectives that students will enjoy achieving? or are most of my objectives dry and boring?

6. Have I included a number of objectives that should help the student develop and retain positive attitudes towards foreign languages? Are there some objectives that everyone can attain easily? Are there too many that are extremely difficult? Will all students be required to reach the difficult ones?

7. Do I have a number of objectives that require group activity, even small group activity, or does the student work individually on all objectives?

8. Do I have a sufficient number of objectives requiring the student to demonstrate his mastery or proficiency orally, or is my curriculum mainly paper and pencil oriented?

9. Is the demonstration of proficiency varied, interesting, and rewarding? Does it appropriately include different types of cognitive behaviors?

10. Have I set up priorities that are feasible for my particular students? Will those objectives that I have chosen help my students reach their goals? Will they help them continue language learning? in our school? elsewhere?

11. Is the set of objectives structured sequentially? Is it logical? Does it make sense?

12. Are the objectives stated clearly so that students, parents, and other teachers know exactly what the learning outcomes should be?

13. Will the attainment of these objectives help the student learn the most important aspects of a foreign language? Will my colleague at the next level accept them and the student who has achieved them?

14. Have I organized the set of objectives so that the student sees why he is asked to do the tasks before him? Do the objectives actually lead to the terminal learnings that I desire?

15. Are the objectives consistent with the goals and purposes and philosophy developed by the school?

16. Is my set of objectives somewhat artificial in nature? Will the student be able to speak and comprehend when he is exposed to "real language"?

17. Are my objectives suitable to the age and maturity of the students for whom they are designed?

18. Do I have a number of objectives that lead the student to free writing or composition and not just to rewrites and translation?

19. Have I included a suitable amount of content for the student for whom I have designed the curriculum?

20. Can the average student achieve all the objectives listed? Is the entire set feasible? What provisions have I made for the below-average student? for the gifted student?

In answering questions 1-9, you may wish to use a checklist or a series of columns where you list each objective under an appropriate heading. You can then tell where you have put the emphasis in your curriculum. It is undoubtedly necessary for some levels to reflect more of one proficiency and other levels to reflect more of others.

You may also wish to have one review sheet for each objective. Then you can record on that page how many of the criteria that particular objective meets. You can then decide whether or not you wish, according to the suggestions made in the Far West Laboratory Materials, to reject the objective, retain it, revise it, or rewrite it entirely.

Once you have decided on your total list, you may want to write an introduction to your objectives in which you summarize your findings. You can list the categories you considered and the numbers of objectives that meet each criteria. You can speak to the matters of guidance, relevance, and feasibility and state why you did not include more or different objectives. If other teachers perusing these materials understand the thought and care that went into the screening, they may value the set considerably more. Of course the real value will be reflected in the intrinsic merit of the set of objectives itself, both for the student's performance and for the larger, program objectives.

XVII. IMPLEMENTING CHANGE

In the professional literature today, particularly in the area of grantsmanship, there is much talk of specific, measurable objectives. Some writers do not make clear whether they are referring to *performance objectives stated in terms of student behavior* or whether they are referring to *program objectives.* It makes sense that the objective of every program should be student learning or student attitude change. Nevertheless, there is an intermediate step which the various agencies that allocate funds have utilized and that is *program objectives. Program objectives tell what a school will do in order to facilitate or bring about student learning.* They do not specify how well the school will perform. The measurement is seldom quantitative but usually involves some form of proof that the stated activity has taken place. It seems logical to me that the writers of the documents would refer to these as *program activities,* for that is what these objectives are in essence. To give an example, if the school has as a goal or purpose that it wishes to improve student performance in the conversational skills of foreign languages, it would devise a program to accomplish this end. A *program* is a group of activities undertaken by student and teacher to help achieve the goals. In this case the goal is for the *school* to improve the conversational skills of students. Administrators, business managers, supervisors, and teachers all have some responsibility, but the specific responsibility of each of these is often ill defined. Program objectives are statements of what the school will accomplish. The proof of the accomplishment is in the measurement. The responsibility for seeing that each objective is carried out must be assigned to a particular individual. For this particular goal—improving conversational skills—the following program objectives could emerge:

1. During the months of September and October all foreign language teachers will enroll in a four-week refresher course offered by the Office of Superintendent of Public Instruction. Measurement: the diploma or certificate awarded will be kept in the departmental files.

2. By September the business office will purchase four tape recorders and four jacks. Measurement: these will be found in the foreign language resource center.

3. By January all foreign language teachers will visit a nearby school which has a model program in the teaching of conversation. Measurement: a written report will be filed with the department chairman.

4. During the last week of August the department chairman will conduct three in-service meetings devoted to small-group work in the classroom. Measurement: minutes of these meetings will be forwarded to the district office.

In the first objective *teachers* bear the responsibility for enrolling. Supervision of this activity is at the department level.

In the second objective the *business office* has the responsibility to purchase the equipment. Again the supervision or check is by the department.

In the third and fourth objectives *teachers* have the responsibility to visit, but a facilitator is probably needed to set up the visits and arrange for substitutes. Supervision at the department level is implied. Notice that no demonstration of proficiency is mentioned in these objectives. They do however clearly assign the responsibility to the administration for doing its part to help the teachers solve the problem. What is not evident is the attitude of the teachers. If they do not wish to change their behavior, they will not profit greatly from any of the activities. Nevertheless, like student performance objectives, these are an improvement over vague statements such as,

"The school will do all it possibly can to help the teachers achieve their goals." No specific responsibility, no outlay of money or time is mentioned in these general statements. In program objectives, the designer of the program states specifically what steps he will take to help achieve the desired outcomes.

Program objectives can represent reality between what is and what should be. There are always some steps that can be taken to solve problems. So often the problem is complex enough that all sit back and wait for others to bring forth a solution. The use of program objectives helps a school or any group chart what it will do and when it will do it.

Program objectives also help schools develop realistic timelines in meeting their objectives. Obviously if teachers wish to improve student conversation skills they must begin early to maintain or update their own skills. By stating deadlines, the program designer helps chart the objectives throughout the school year, and valuable time is not lost because other activities intervene.

The sum total of the program objectives represents a course of action for achieving a certain goal. The objectives should stem from an assessment of needs. This assessment should be a discussion and consideration of all the problems facing the department or the school, and from these myriad problems one area should be selected as the need on which the program will be based. If more than one area of need is included, the program becomes more complex, but then most school programs prove to be complex. The selection of a single area of need and the structuring of a set of program objectives help the school to move more logically into the area of problem solving.

There is another ingredient needed here, and that is evaluation. At the end of the time allotment, the program objectives should be evaluated. The following questions should be raised and answered:

1. Were all the objectives reached? By the time indicated? If not, why not?

2. If all the program objectives were met, was the problem solved? If not, what aspect of it still needs solving? What objectives did not prove successful in solving the problem? Why? What alternatives could be suggested that would probably help solve the problem?

3. Can the alternatives mentioned in 2 above be translated into program objectives?

As a result of these considerations the following action could ensue:

1. The objectives were achieved, the problem was solved, and the program does not need to be continued. Attention can be focused on some other aspect of the program.

2. The objectives were achieved, the program was successful, the problem was solved, but a new problem emerged (perhaps that of maintaining the new program) which will have to be solved.

3. The objectives were reached, but the problem was not solved. If the problem still has high priority, then a new set of program objectives should emerge. If the problem has now been assigned a lower priority, the program may be abandoned.

4. The program objectives were not reached, but the problem was solved anyway. There is no need to continue the program.

5. The program objectives were not reached, and the problem was not solved. If the problem has high priority, the objectives should be rescheduled for the next year. Perhaps some can be deleted and others added, if the program designers so choose.

Program objectives provide effective communication between departments and administration. Frequently one hears teachers say, "The administration doesn't care about foreign languages. It doesn't do anything about them." Often the administration is not in a position to decide what should be done for foreign languages. Few administrators come from this area, many have only a vague idea about the problems involved, and they are not always adept at suggesting effective means of change. It is far from the truth to suppose that these administrators do not wish to see improvements in this area. Instead of just asking for more money and smaller class size, departments should draw up programs focusing on one specific area of need. They should then write a series of program objectives. These objectives should reflect the responsibility of all those concerned: department chairmen, teachers, guidance counselors, etc. If possible the program development should include representatives from these various groups. When the plan is presented to the administration, it will then be clear what is expected, when, and from whom. Now the decision makers can determine what their commitment to the project should be. If the planning has been realistic, there is a good chance that the program will be adopted. An honest evaluation of the program at the end of the time indicated provides a good rationale for asking for further funds, personnel, etc. as through PPBS.

PPBS stands for Planning, Programming, Budgeting System. This is a movement or system that attempts to allot *funds and resources,* including personnel, for the attainment of *programs* that are designed to help students reach specific measurable *performance objectives.* At the end of a designated period of time *student performance* is measured. *Program effectiveness* is assessed upon the basis of this student performance, and recommendations for improvement are made. It is possible that during the time the program is in operation new *needs* will have arisen. These needs, together with the original needs, must now be *assessed.* New statements of student performance and new programs will be proposed. Some of the parts of the "new" programs will undoubtedly be the redevelopment of the previous programs. Funds and resources will then be redistributed. The cycle is a dynamic process and can be diagrammed as follows:

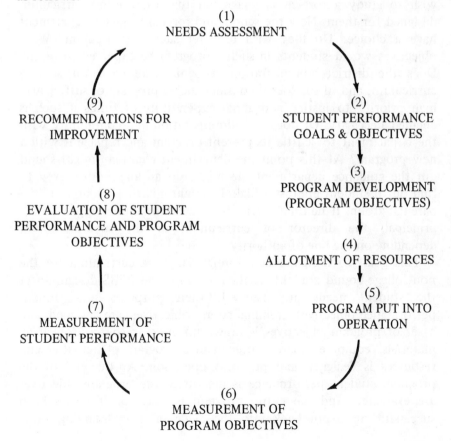

(1)
NEEDS ASSESSMENT

(9)
RECOMMENDATIONS FOR
IMPROVEMENT

(2)
STUDENT PERFORMANCE
GOALS & OBJECTIVES

(3)
PROGRAM DEVELOPMENT
(PROGRAM OBJECTIVES)

(8)
EVALUATION OF STUDENT
PERFORMANCE AND PROGRAM
OBJECTIVES

(4)
ALLOTMENT OF RESOURCES

(7)
MEASUREMENT OF
STUDENT PERFORMANCE

(5)
PROGRAM PUT INTO
OPERATION

(6)
MEASUREMENT OF
PROGRAM OBJECTIVES

Let us consider one example of how PPBS works. A school may have as one of its goals:

> . . . to provide an opportunity for all students to learn how peoples and cultures differ.

The foreign language department may have as its goal:

> . . . to provide an opportunity for college-bound students to study a foreign language and to learn from this study how peoples and cultures differ.

At this point PPBS almost automatically requires a needs assessment. Surveys, information from the community, feedback from guidance counselors and from students may indicate that this goal should be maintained since a large percentage of students are college bound. These same sources of information may indicate that other students wish to study a foreign language but that there is no curriculum designed for them. Now the school and foreign language department have a choice: Do they wish to offer such a curriculum? What objectives would students in such a program be expected to reach? Does the district administration recognize the need for such a curriculum, and, if so, does it consider such a program of sufficiently high priority to justify additional expenditure of funds if such is deemed necessary. Or does the administration and community wish the department to scuttle its present program and replace it with a new program? At this point the department chairman might sound out the guidance department; he might do an all-school survey to find out if student interest is high; he might make a presentation to a parents' group. If he finds sufficient interest, he should approach the principal, the director of curriculum, or the superintendent, depending on the line of authority.

This goal, to design a new foreign language curriculum for the non-college-bound student, is then set into the PPBS design. After the student needs are assessed, their purposes and student performance objectives (terminal course objectives) are designed, and a set of program objectives is drawn up. Next, resources (teachers, materials, equipment) are alloted, and a program of activities and resources is designed and put into operation. At the end of the program, student performance is measured, the program objectives are evaluated, and the entire program is assessed. If it has been successful, it is put back into the cycle on a maintaining basis.

Perhaps more, perhaps fewer resources will be required to maintain the program. If it was developed on a small scale and on an experimental basis, more funds will be needed to expand and implement the program. Normally, however, one expects the developmental stage to be the more costly.

In short, PPBS is a means of helping schools set objectives, determine priorities, decide on a plan of action, measure the results, evaluate the entire package, and make future decisions. It also allows a school to see the relationship between money and results. We all know that money alone does not buy performance, but it frequently helps. It is my opinion that PPBS *can* help foreign language instruction. Many other academic and nonacademic areas are more costly than foreign languages, and some of them produce fewer results. The real secret lies first in devising meaningful and realistic student performance objectives, then in designing good program objectives, and finally in demonstrating our success to all. We should then be in a better position to get our "slice of the pie," including our selection of the best textbooks.

XVIII. TEXTBOOKS
and RESOURCES

Textbook selection is a complex process. Problems differ at the various levels. In most elementary and junior high schools, and in some high schools, the school purchases the texts. In other high schools, in junior colleges, and in colleges, students purchase texts. Since problems differ at the various levels, I shall deal with secondary schools, junior colleges, and colleges separately.

In the spring of the year in most secondary schools there is a big rush to select textbooks for the coming year. In some systems a committee is appointed and charged with the task of reviewing and selecting all textbooks. In other systems all the teachers are personally involved in the review and selection. Practices vary, of course, and in states where there are state-adopted texts, a state committee, sometimes clouded in secrecy to protect the committee members from undue persuasion, selects either one book or a slate of three to five texts from which schools or teachers may choose. It little matters what the procedure, the frustrations are common. No single selection will please everybody. Each text possesses strengths and weaknesses; there is rarely a single "star." No matter how much objectivity the selectors exercise, it is difficult for them to keep their personal biases divorced from the selection process. Some real progress has been made; checklists of various kinds have appeared that help teachers to ask the "right" questions. These are certainly valuable aids. Nevertheless, the most important questions can hardly be raised and answered by a checklist. It is this writer's contention that the most valid answers are to be found by consulting the teacher's or the system's performance objectives.

In the previous chapter we discussed the difference between program objectives and student performance objectives. I suggest that textbook committees begin their review by consulting the school and the departmental goals. If one of the goals is to open foreign language study to all students, the committee must look for books that are written at a lower reading level, and they must also consider the format of the book. Is it written in segments that will not discourage students who are not highly self-motivated? These broad goals or objectives will help the committee select texts to review thoroughly. *Committee time must be considered.* Too often committee members spend an inordinate amount of time reviewing one set of materials and give only a cursory review to another. They may be misled by such features as print or type styles, illustrations or pictures. These are not unimportant from a motivational point of view, but they should not be the prime basis of review. If a committee selects a limited number of texts that seem compatible with the goals and objectives, then the committee can spend its time more effectively reviewing these and charting them to see whether or not they carry out the department's performance objectives.

Once the committee is set for this second round of reviewing it should have in front of it at all times the specific set of performance objectives—both the terminal course objectives and the learning objectives. A chart should be constructed so that the following information can be inserted:

1. *Learning Objective One* The student shall imitate the vowel sounds of Spanish by repeating these sounds accurately when he hears them on a tape or spoken by his teacher. These sounds may be in known or unknown words.
Criterion: 90% correct.
   a. Does the set of materials provide any material for teaching the vowel sounds? _____

b. Does the set of materials contain

tapes? _____

tapes that teach the vowel sounds? _____

tapes that test the vowel sounds? _____

c. Does the teaching of the vowel sounds appear at an appropriate time slot in the curriculum, or will the text or material have to be adjusted?

d. Is the amount of material sufficient to help the student meet the performance objectives, or will the teacher have to supplement the material?

e. Is this material presented in an appealing way to students, or is it likely to discourage students?

f. Is the material suited for

bright, highly motivated students? _____

the average student in the class? _____

the youngster who may have some learning problems? _____

g. Is there too much material on this particular objective? Will teachers have to delete some of the material?

Using the above answers, rate the set of materials as it pertains to this objective.

1. Implements the objective very well.

2. Implements the objective well but will need some adaptation.

3. Can implement the objective if there is a great deal of adaptation.

4. Contains some material that will help implement the objective, but teachers will have to write a supplementary unit.

5. Does not implement the objective.

It is obvious that such a review measures a text to the extent that it does or does not help to implement a specific set of objectives. I maintain that this is the basis on which materials should be selected. It does not, of course, answer the question as to whether or not the set of objectives is in itself a good set of objectives. But only the writers or users of the objectives are in a position to consider that question. If in reviewing various sets of materials a committee finds that its own set of objectives does not cover some aspect of language learning, it may want to raise the question as to whether or not these aspects should be included in the curriculum. However, it is obvious that at this point the teachers and the curriculum designers are raising and answering questions. They are not blindly assuming that something should be in the curriculum because certain authors, editors, and publishers assumed that it should be there. A committee should also consider the content and the organization of the book or, in other words, its scope and sequence. If two texts are judged comparable in facilitating the implementation of the terminal course and learning objectives, then some consideration should be paid to the order in which the materials appear. Attention must also be paid to the vocabulary and points of structure selected by the authors.

Textbooks should be selected to meet the specific needs of specific students in a specific place at a specific time. Students change, teachers change, and times change. Education is an unending effort to match teaching strategies, materials, and students. This is in no way meant to imply that the teacher is not important in the selection of a textbook. But most teachers want to choose a text that will help them teach *students* better. If they select a text which they like but which does not help their students learn, they will soon become disillusioned with the text and may even become disillusioned with teaching. This happens many times; teachers select a text which looks interesting and intriguing to them, then try it and find out that the text does not "teach" very well. This has led schools to adopt pilot systems where the text is tried in one or two classes to see if it meets the needs of the students in that system. When a text is adopted for a pilot program, those adopting it should continue to rate the text according to how well the text helps students to meet the specific performance objectives. This gives teachers a sound basis to judge whether or not the text should be kept or discontinued.

In systems where some attempt is being made to individualize, the selection of materials is extremely important. Once the decision has been made to individualize, teachers must decide whether or not they wish to individualize rate, materials, or objectives. To date most systems have opted to individualize rate. This has great implications for the choice of materials. Texts must be selected that enable teachers to make the curriculum flexible without causing them to rewrite the text completely. It is of prime importance that they have enough drill material, exercises, tests, and quizzes. Caution should be exercised to include a section in the review chart that deals with this aspect.

If teachers elect to individualize objectives, the text should first be examined to see if it provides sufficient material to meet the needs of various types of students. If teachers have samples of the objectives they wish to assign students, they can rate the text by some system such as the one mentioned above. It is highly unlikely that one set of materials will be sufficient for all the objectives if their decision is to vary objectives for both skill and content. Teachers may find that it is easier to work with multiple sets of materials. This is not so formidable as it sounds. For years teachers have selected separate readers for levels I and II. They have also selected films to supplement books and materials that did not contain sufficient audio-visual materials. They also have on occasion used a workbook to reinforce the grammatical concepts presented in the basic text.

Foreign language departments frequently complain that their budgets are cut so that they cannot acquire those materials they need to teach their students properly. Administrators reply to these charges by saying that there is no correlation between the materials teachers claim to need and student performance. A convincing argument would be to show an administrator a chart such as the one mentioned above so that he may see for himself how the present materials fail to implement student performance objectives and how the proposed set of materials would do this much better. When he sees that the teachers have spent time deciding on a text that is suitable for their specific objectives he will be more convinced of the merit of such a change. In the previous chapter we spoke of PPBS. Such a system clearly relates the purchase of materials to student achievement. As was stated in the previous chapter, the type of student achievement that should be measured is that defined by teachers. Similarly, the types of materials needed to help students reach the objectives should be set forth by teachers. The costs should be put into proper perspective. Let us linger for a moment in a consideration of budgets and costs.

If a foreign language teacher did not think his subject the most important one in the curriculum, he would probably be unique among teachers. One cannot devote his life to a subject without feeling that it is of prime importance. This is not to say that every foreign language teacher would wish to automatically banish all other subjects from the curriculum. It is rather to imply that decisions which adversely affect foreign languages are not easily accepted by foreign language teachers. Administrators frequently have to choose between the needs of various disciplines. This is not an easy task; one does not like to sit in judgment on the value of one discipline over another. Nevertheless, in practical matters such as the allotment of budgets, the assignment of classrooms, the place in the schedule, and the number of teachers to be assigned, the administrator must remember the old adage that you cannot spend the same money twice. When he has to make a decision he prefers to make that decision as objectively as possible. He asks himself, "Where will this money (classroom, schedule, teacher) do the greatest amount of good for the greatest number of students?" If a department is united, knows what it wants, has documentation to show that it has studied various alternatives and has come to a common decision that what is in its proposal is right and valid for its students, it can make a much more convincing case than a group that has not put forward this effort.

Foreign language teachers are often quite individualistic. This is as it should be, but there is a time to stand united. There is a time to reach agreement on matters such as textbooks so that a united front can be presented to the administration. Personal and emotional frustrations can be minimized if teachers make an objective effort to set forth the criteria they are looking for in materials, to review those materials thoroughly, and to interpret the results of their investigations to the administration.

The first part of this chapter has been addressed to secondary and elementary school teachers. The second and third parts are addressed to junior college and college teachers. The latter operate in a different sphere and have different pressures upon them. Let us first look at the circumstances of the junior college.

The junior college was designed to meet the specific needs of a student population that was not ready or willing to attempt the work of the four-year college at the time of graduation from high school. This may not be true of all today's junior college students across the country. It is true, however, that many students find access to junior colleges easier than access to four-year colleges. While I believe that, in the past three to five years, many capable students have elected to attend junior colleges primarily because they did not have the funds to go away to school, the junior college has a basic responsibility to students who need remedial programs, to students whose interests are not met in the four-year college, and to students who are looking for specific vocational training. It is inevitable that a foreign language department at a junior college should have a different mission from the comparable department in a four-year liberal arts college or university.

It is this writer's observation that few publishers have yet produced appropriate materials for use at this level. The junior college is usually forced to choose between inappropriate high school texts and inappropriate college texts. The junior college teacher is also confronted with the problems of the affective domain. How will his students respond to using materials that are not "college" materials? Their response represents a genuine difficulty since many students entering junior colleges lack a reading skill commensurate with the materials they are expected to use. I believe that it is imperative that teachers at this level define performance objectives for their students. I think that they must be very realistic in defining the purposes on which these performance objectives will be based. Some of the questions they should raise are:

1. Is the program designed primarily for students who have never studied a foreign language or for those who have already had foreign language training in high school? In other words, is it remedial in nature or is it a beginning sequence?

2. At the end of two years of study at the junior college, does the teacher expect all, the majority, or only a few to be able to enter third year at the university?

3. Is the purpose of the foreign language program to help students acquire a speaking knowledge of the foreign language or to prepare them for the study of literature at the college level?

4. Are there any vocational purposes to the junior college program? Is there any attempt to coordinate programs with those in other departments?

Only after these questions have been answered should teachers write a set of student performance objectives. The department may find that it has to provide multiple programs to meet the needs of each set of students mentioned above. It may, in fact, be that the department will find it desirable to individualize its program to meet the needs of various groups of students, for unless it is individualized, no single program is likely to meet the various needs of all students.

Junior college teachers should, more than ever, continue to lobby for books that are prepared to meet their specific needs. In the meantime they, above all other teachers, should select books and materials that best meet the specific performance objectives of their students. They may wish to examine programmed, self-pacing and self-instructional materials, although they will not want to have students work independently at all times. If they have three different ability groups in the same class they may want to use more small-group instruction and different sets of performance objectives. The materials for one group of students may need to be quite different in design from those used by other groups. Junior college students, unlike students in the secondary school, are further along in their career choices. Many of them have been forced to face realistically the fact that they may not be able to complete a degree within a four-year period. Teachers on occasion may have to point out to certain students that a given text aimed at high school students may be more appropriate for them than a comparable college text.

The junior college teacher must convince his students that learning is a life-long process and that what the student learns now can be extended at a later date. The junior college student is apt to want to acquire mastery of one language skill only, and the teacher had best design a set of objectives and choose a set of materials that will help this student meet the objectives of that skill. He may have to blend a low level of skill mastery with a higher level of content, since the maturity of the junior college student is greater than that of many high school students.

To sum up, it is of great importance that the junior college teacher design a set of objectives for his students; he may in fact, be forced to design several sets of objectives for his students if they differ radically in interests, abilities, and needs. He must then select a wide range of materials that meet these various objectives, and he should base this selection on whether or not the materials will help the student reach the designated objectives. He should not forget the possible effects of certain types of material on his students, but he should explain to the students that, in his opinion, for this particular objective or set of objectives, the materials suggested will best help them learn. He may want to offer several types of materials from which students can select, but he will at all times want to guide and advise students so that they will be successful in reaching the objectives. If a student experiences success at this level, he will be more inclined to continue his foreign language learning in the future.

College textbook selection is frequently much simpler than the selection of textbooks at the secondary level. First of all, college professors are free to change books as frequently as they wish. They do not have the usual problems of adoptions, resale, etc., that occur when a school system purchases texts. They also can count on a more sophisticated student with a higher maturity level. There are, however, different problems which plague the college professor.

First of all, the college professor must select a book that can be covered in the appropriate time span. If he is teaching language skills, he must look for a book that covers all the essential points. In addition, he must select a book that is appropriate to the adult world, one that differs from the secondary texts.

While the above considerations must play a part, the selection of a college textbook should still be based on the same premise as that of a secondary text or junior college text, namely, which book will help the students best achieve the stated performance objectives? All the rest are secondary considerations. It matters not that the book is written by distinguished scholars if students cannot read and understand it. It matters not if the book covers all the salient points if students cannot possibly master those points in the time alloted. It matters not if it is appropriate to the adult world if students do not have sufficient skills to learn from it.

Not all college students are equal in linguistic proficiency, in the basic native-language skills of reading and writing, or in aptitude. Perhaps in college, more than anywhere else, there needs to be multiple sets of materials to match the skills of the learner. The current literature tells us that open admissions are now a reality, that admission to college may depend primarily on the student's ability to pay, especially in the case of the small private college. Thus the professor can no longer assume that the student either must "measure up" or be failed, or he will soon be out of business. He can also no longer assume that the topics which interest him, his special areas of research, are important to every student. With the disappearance of the language requirement, students are electing those courses that have relevance for them and *those courses in which they feel that they can succeed.* The judicious choice of a text at the college level can contribute to the feeling of success and can make the professor's task easier. Assuming that the professor has set forth the objectives for his students, that he has reviewed these objectives and has found them feasible and relevant, he should ask himself the following questions as he considers possible texts:

1. What is the reading level presupposed by this text? (If he does not know this, he can sample student performance by asking one of his classes to read a passage in class and answer some questions using only the text. To be sure, this would have to take place in the Spring term of the previous year.)

2. Can students study this text independently? Are the explanations clear, or do they depend upon a teacher's interpretation? If the explanations are scanty in places, are there other resources (books, handouts, etc.) that would help the student work independently?

3. Does the book offer appropriate conversational materials and tapes if the course is at a beginning or intermediate level? Where and how will the student learn to pronounce? to speak? If he is to go to the language laboratory, are materials available that will indicate clearly to him what he is to do and why?

4. Does the text appeal to the young adult? Is it in tune with the times? Is the book attractive to look at? Does it contain material that is mature enough for the student but still structurally accessible to him?

In most college courses the student is expected to do a great deal of independent work. It is appropriate that when a student enters college he should work more independently than when he was in high school, that he should assume a greater measure of responsibility for his own learning, but this in no way implies that he does not need a teacher. If colleges are now accepting students from the entire ability spectrum, the college must recognize that it has to meet different sets of student needs. It must structure independent learning more than it did previously. It must guide students more effectively. Students resent paying for a text that does not help them to reach the course objectives and whose study does not result in a higher grade for them. Therefore the text itself can be an indirect cause of decreasing student enrollment.

As students differ more widely in ability, the resources they use must also differ widely. This in no way implies that more than one text need be required in a course. It *does* imply that copies of other texts, perhaps even some secondary school-level texts, need to be available to the student in case he encounters difficulty. It also implies that college instructors may have to become more interested and more involved in student learning processes than they have been previously, and that they will need to select materials for various types of students who may be enrolled in the same class.

It stands to reason that these observations are more applicable to the early stages of language learning. Nevertheless, they also have some application at the upper levels where departments have to compete for student enrollments. Textbooks and resources which help the student learn the important elements of the course are of great assistance in helping a student decide whether to continue enrolling in courses in the subject area. Texts that may be beautifully written but that do not help the student achieve the objectives on which he is being graded do little to build motivation to continue studying. Hence it would be wise for the college instructor to set forth his objectives, select texts that help the student reach the objectives, and measure the student's performance in terms of those objectives. The selection of a text should always *serve* the program, not *determine* the program.

XIX. CAREER EDUCATION

Recently a new topic, career education, has captured the interest of educators. It has been assigned a top educational priority by the federal government, and many states are beginning to mandate career education as part of every school curriculum. One might assume that, like health education or consumer education, it would simply be offered as one more course to be added to the existing curricular pile. However, such is not the case. If current thinking is implemented, career education will become *a required part of every subject*. Career education will begin in kindergarten and will extend at least through the first two years of college. This is one reason for including some mention of it in this book. The second reason is a belief on my part that a judicious selection of performance objectives dealing with careers can help the foreign language curriculum, the student, and our profession.

It might be well to examine first of all some definitions of career education and some misconceptions about it. Then we will consider some possible career-oriented performance objectives that would be appropriate to foreign languages. In the book entitled *Career Education: What It Is and How to Do It* (Kenneth B. Hoyt, *et al.*, 1972), two definitions are offered. Hoyt (p. 1) defines it as "the total effort of public education and the community aimed at helping all individuals to become familiar with the values of a work-oriented society, and to integrate these values into their personal value systems, and to implement these values into their lives in such a way that work becomes possible, meaningful, and satisfying to each individual." Evans (p. 1) sees it as "the total effort of the community to develop a personally satisfying succession of opportunities for service through work, paid or unpaid, extending throughout life." One fact is clear: career education is not synonymous with vocational education, although vocational education is a part of it. Career education implies the development of all an individual's talents, the development of self-awareness of those talents (and their corresponding limitations), the development of a knowledge of what careers are in demand today and what, according to our best projections, will be in demand ten years from now. It implies developing a flexibility in students so that, if they find that the career for which they are preparing themselves is no longer in vogue, they will be able to adapt themselves and their talents to a different job that is in demand.

Many foreign language specialists have been wary of career education because they fear that it will detract from an emphasis on the humanistic value of foreign languages. I feel, on the contrary, that if we adhere to the broad definitions given above, career education is quite compatible with the goals—humanistic and pragmatic—that we have promulgated in the past. Let us take another look at the various facets of career education that have been proposed by some writers. First of all, in the elementary grades children should develop *career awareness*—that is, they should develop an awareness of jobs that people around them perform. They should also be made aware of which careers can utilize the skills and content that they, in these early grades, are now learning. A simplistic example of this is for the second grade teacher to point out that the department store clerk must write the amounts of purchases legibly so that the company will bill the person for the correct amount. Another would be that the mailman must be able to read correctly or he will deliver letters to the wrong house. It is hoped by the proponents of career education that this will make all school subjects seem more relevant to the learner. In junior high school and high school there should be an emphasis on careers which presuppose the subject being studied, careers which utilize the subject as an ancillary skill, or careers which are pursued primarily by people who have reaped the humanistic benefits that the study of that particular subject can offer.

The following performance objectives show how career awareness may be inserted into a foreign language program:

1. The student shall explain how any two of the six persons listed might find knowledge of a foreign language especially useful: actress, taxi driver, hotel clerk, waiter, opera singer, secretary in an international business firm. In two paragraphs he will explain what types of linguistic skills the person would need for his profession (e.g., pronunciation, silent reading, translation, oral comprehension, oral response, etc.).

2. Given a one-page letter of request written in German for an item of merchandise which is produced in varying sizes and shapes, the student will translate the specific request into English in writing and include the American equivalents for measurements. He will make no more than two errors in content.

3. Given standard application forms for an airline ticket and flight insurance, the student will complete the necessary information in Spanish as given to him by a classmate posing as non-English speaking. The form will contain no more than three errors in vocabulary.

4. Given a brief English description of a robbery, a student will pose as a Spanish-speaking witness, reporting the robbery to a classmate posing as a local law-enforcement agent. The report will be filed in English by the "policeman." The witness may make no more than three errors of omission and/or accuracy of content and no more than five in structure and vocabulary. The policeman may make no more than two errors in content.

5. Given an anatomical chart with the Latin names of ten bones, muscles, or organs indicated, the student will render the names into English, pointing out the appropriateness of the Latin terminology, with no more than two errors in the interpretation of the Latin.

Obviously these objectives would be appropriate at widely different course levels, and there are many other types that would serve equally well.

As we mentioned in the chapter dealing with the affective domain and values, there are many topics that can make our present curricula more relevant and interesting to the learner. These in no way need interfere with the development of skills and the development of attitudes. One of the components of career education is self-awareness, that is, coming to know one's own talents. If, in the study of a foreign language, the student becomes aware of the fact that he likes to imitate sound, that he can learn to deal with people who are different from himself, that he can accept and enjoy another culture and can understand another value system, he will have acquired some knowledge of himself that may help when he selects a life occupation. This knowledge may also set him apart from others and give him a unique quality.

In another stage of career education, students should be introduced to the specifics of certain careers. We have done little with this preparation, except at a superficial level, in foreign languages. For example, airline stewardesses need to know how to pronounce a foreign language correctly more than they need other linguistic skills. Much of what they have to communicate is written for them on cards, and they read it. This is not to deny that they should also know how to ask some basic questions and to communicate basic information in an emergency. It also does not deny that many are accomplished linguists, but it does mean that large numbers of them are proficient in one area of language skills without being so, or have to be so, in all areas. Actresses, taxi drivers, and hotel employees are also frequently fluent in only a very limited, specialized vocabulary, but even that limited vocabulary is of great value to them. As the United States becomes a greater attraction for the foreign tourist, a smattering of a foreign language can become increasingly valuable as an ancillary career skill.

XX. HUMANIZATION or DEHUMANIZATION?

As we stated in the first chapter of this book, performance objectives are not new; they have grown out of the past. They have been tried before. Now, owing to various influences, they have reappeared on the educational scene. The question now becomes: Will they endure? Will they enhance education? Or will they, too, pass and be forgotten? If time and situation affect the implementation of an idea, then it is logical to assume that an idea could flourish in one time and in one place where it may have failed previously. Whether an idea will actually endure depends on a number of factors:

1. Does the idea have basic merit?
2. Will the idea help solve the problems of the day?
3. Do the advantages outweigh the disadvantages?
4. Are there more proponents than opponents of the idea?
5. Are the proponents of the idea persuasive and reasonable or do they try to foist the idea on an unwilling public?
6. Are circumstances such that the idea can flourish?

The *present* age with its demands for accountability and relevance, with its move towards the individualization of instruction and open-access campuses, should prove to be a more fertile age for performance objectives than was the past. I believe that we have learned enough about education, people, and group processes to allow us to implement performance objectives more effectively at this point in time than we were able to do in the past. Each time an old idea comes around again it has a better chance of success if its users have learned from past experience. There is much in the present, and perhaps in the future, that makes performance objectives particularly attractive. One may decry accountability, protest against PPBS, object to the fact that the U.S. Office of Education and state agencies require the use of objectives, but the truth of the matter is that most schools need federal funding; they therefore have little choice as to whether or not they like performance objectives if they wish to qualify for these grants. As the public begins to demand an accounting of the money it has granted to the schools, it will ask to see results. Sometimes the information that is said to measure performance is at best sketchy, sporadic, and unreliable. Even if performance objectives sometimes leave much to be desired, the fact that *teachers* are asked to write them, that *teachers* are asked to determine the mastery level, and that *teachers* are asked to choose the evaluation tools, makes them a better choice, in my opinion, than the indiscriminate use of achievement tests that has been the pattern in many places.

As we look to the future we can be sure that our society will retain a measure of mobility. This will call for greater articulation as students move from one school system to the next. There will be many more transfer students than previously. If one has a record of the objectives a student has achieved, the transfer and the phase-in should be considerably easier than they have been in the past.

At present the opponents of performance objectives claim that objectives dehumanize education. Some may feel that the dehumanization has already begun. I submit that the humanizing or dehumanizing of anything depends on the *individual*—be it student or teacher. There is no denying the fact that many systems which have implemented performance curricula have made numerous mistakes. Any change will produce mistakes, because systems and teachers have to learn a new *modus operandi*. It does not follow that these mistakes must endure. It is dehumanizing for a teacher to give a student a set of performance objectives and then not expect to see him again for a month. It is dehumanizing if the teacher expects to do no instructing, no interacting with the student, but there are many dehumanizing qualities to some *traditional* teaching as well. Is it not dehumanizing to ask a student to repeat *ad nauseaum* work he has already mastered? Is it not dehumanizing to put a student through a class which he cannot understand and where he is doomed to failure because he does not have sufficient entry skills or background? Is it not dehumanizing to watch a teacher insult a child and cause him to hate to come to class because the teacher humiliates him each day? Yet it would be ridiculous to condemn all traditional teaching because these acts are committed by some teachers. It is equally unfair to condemn a movement because a few people use it badly. The charge that the use of performance objectives resembles putting rats through mazes is usually most inappropriate. It is within the creativity, imagination, and artistry of every teacher to devise *several ways* of meeting most performance objectives. In fact if performance objectives are well implemented they should offer the student a wide variety of activities and resources that he can use in order to reach the objective. This allows (or can allow) him a choice; he can follow his own learning style. If the class presentation does not work for him, or if he is absent, he can engage in other activities that should help him to reach the objective. The use of self-tests, the practice of telling the student what concepts and skills he should master, makes learning much more human and much less capricious. I would be the first to grant that if the student does not meet with other students regularly, if he does not have frequent interaction with the teacher, he may feel isolated and dehumanized. While the use of performance objectives may allow the above two practices, their use in no way requires them, nor should it do so.

I would also add that there are some "mazes" which a student needs to enter if he wishes to learn to speak a language, and I suggest that these "mazes" be put into segments of programmed learning. I have suggested that the best curriculum is one which allows the student some voice in selecting which performance objectives he will reach. If a student understands the nature of performance objectives, he can at certain points in his learning write some for himself. This is what a researcher, a writer, an artist must do. The teacher can then help him by suggesting activities and resources that should best help him reach the objective.

A much more valid objection is that we cannot always specify in advance what a student's performance will be. Even in the areas of arts, such as a musical competition, however, judges know what they intend to look for, what criteria merit praise. What they do, however, is to leave room for the unexpected. When an English teacher assigns a poem to be written, he cannot specify in advance the quality that he will receive, but he can share with the student those qualities or characteristics that he knows he will look for in the poem. These expressive areas are difficult, but they do not comprise all or even the majority of learning in schools today. Perhaps they should occupy a greater part of the curriculum than they now do. In the majority of our courses student performance is indeed predicted in advance *in the teacher's mind,* but it is not shared with the student, and the student does not always have the maturity, insight, and judgment to perceive what the teacher wants. He often learns the wrong thing, and he suffers for this in his evaluation. He may not be able to continue the study of the subject because he studied the wrong material and did not know what the teacher expected of him.

It is also true that one cannot guarantee that every student will achieve every objective. We do not know in advance who will produce the masterpiece, but this does not deny the validity of specifying performance in advance. I cannot accept the idea that teachers do not have specific ideas about how various types of instruction affect students. If we do not know what we *expect* the student to learn in the course, I do not see how we can plan any course for him, or any learning. Everything then becomes a chance occurrence. It is equally true that no single person, no single performance objective, no set of performance objectives should try to determine *everything* a student will learn. To do so would be ridiculous.

Teachers, too, are the victims of caprice. Frequently someone will decide to evaluate a teacher's performance by testing his students. If the teacher has adopted objectives that differ from the supervisor's, then the teacher is judged to be incompetent when in reality he is simply working towards different objectives. Emotional arguments can often be solved if one can state what it is that he wishes his students to be able to do at the end of the course.

I can accept the objection that there is no agreement among language specialists as to what are the best outcomes for students, but I maintain that *every teacher does expect certain outcomes for his students.* The fact there is no agreement nationally does not constitute a basis for saying that we as individuals should not predict outcomes or try to specify student behavior in advance. In fact, by using performance objectives, and by individualizing these objectives for students, we give the student much more voice in the choice of his goals than we do when we put him into a classroom and teach him one curriculum into which he has little or no input. At least he has the knowledge of what will be expected of him, and he can select his courses more wisely. Throughout this book I have made a plea for student choice in learning. I think it is essential that the teacher know what he is teaching or going to teach, that he share this information with prospective students, and that students have some voice in the choice of objectives. We should also let the student know which activities in our opinion will lead to the achievement of certain objectives. We may likewise have to motivate or persuade the student to reach some objectives he does not care to reach because these are essential steps towards objectives he does wish to reach.

I believe that the future will hold many more choices for students and that they will become real partners in the educational enterprise. I think that they will demand to know what is in a particular course, what the requirements or objectives are, and to what level of mastery they will need to perform. This will be particularly true of the drop out or the stop out who returns and wishes to continue his learning.

An interesting objection to performance objectives is that they put the emphasis on attainment of the goal and take it off the process of arriving at the goal (Grittner, 1972, p. 57). If by this the writer means that how we learn a specific bit of information is made less important than learning the information, I would agree and repeat my claim that performance objectives put the emphasis on outcomes while allowing for a plethora of learning styles and methods. If, however, he is implying that the process of learning a language is deemphasized by the use of performance objectives, then I take exception. *I think that the most important task of all is learning how to learn.* The most valuable lesson to be learned from studying Spanish is how to learn a language. I maintain also that *there are many acceptable ways to learn.* In the language profession we have for too long been seduced by *method* when we should have been considering *methods.* There is also the matter of attitude. I agree that no amount of subject matter content can compete with poor attitudes. If a method is efficient but causes the student to hate the subject and leave it, then the method should be avoided for that particular student. The process of learning does play a great part in the development of attitudes. Establishing sound performance objectives should in no way impede the use of good methods; rather, establishing such objectives should facilitate the use of appropriate methods, It is well to remember, too, that the outcomes of learning are not always the amount of content that the person has mastered; it may be that little subject matter is required but that skill development is emphasized.

Some objections center around the content of performance objectives. Frank Grittner is quite right when he says that all content becomes obsolete and that the performance objectives we write today will one day have to be revised (1972, p. 57). Revision is to be expected. Even interpretations of literature become obsolete and have to be reshaped. Teachers, therefore, will surely, from time to time, have to review and revise their objectives. They should do this with the course plans, tests, etc., that they use in traditional classes as well. Nevertheless, if the performance objectives are well written the content can be revised without a great deal of difficulty. This is especially true if the group has used the goal refinement system. If one has converted a textbook into performance terms, he will have to write a new set of objectives when he changes texts. If he has used a text to implement the objectives, however, then he need only revise the resources when he changes books.

Another valid objection is that most performance objectives center around grammar, reading and writing, and vocabulary. This is sad but true; however, it is a natural *first stage* of development in most classrooms. When one is learning a new process he experiments with it under the easiest circumstances. When one acquires a measure of proficiency he can then move into the more difficult areas. I have emphasized throughout this book that teachers must balance the set of objectives they write and must have an appropriate number of objectives dealing with conversation skills and with culture.

Imbalance in curriculum is not necessarily limited to performance curricula; the same imbalance exists in many traditional classes. Tests are often paper and pencil tests heavily centered around grammar and vocabulary, and culture is a neglected portion of the curriculum.

One of the reasons that performance objectives will endure is that they reveal weaknesses in a curriculum. Some critics have stated that curricula written in performance terms are inferior to curricula that are not so stated. This may in part actually be true, but usually the inferiority is only apparent: the writing or translation of a curriculum into performance terms *reveals* weaknesses that were in the curriculum all the time. Most curricula that are not written in performance terms specify very little that is taught and tested. They are broad and general, and they sound pleasing to the ear. There is frequently a wide divergence between what is found in the guide and what is done in the classroom.

If performance objectives are to endure, teachers must accept them. We can divide the objections raised by teachers into several categories. First of all there are objections that center around the teacher's freedom. Many teachers feel that they should be free to "do their own thing." They feel that teaching is an individualistic act, that there should be no controls or restraints imposed on them. In the past this has often been true, and teachers see no reason for this freedom to disappear. They want to teach what they want to teach when they want to teach it. They feel that the use of performance objectives will cause them to lose the spontaneity which they have previously enjoyed. They fear that the "magic moments" of the classroom—those in which a teacher and student move closer to each other, when a common task envelops both in excitement—will disappear entirely. There is the fear that all of their teaching will be centered around putting information into students' heads and that the "essence of teaching" will be lost. There is, again, a measure of truth in these objections. I do grant that performance objectives, by lending direction to a course, may cause it to become something other than what the teacher would prefer to do from day to day. Nevertheless, there is no rule requiring a teacher to teach only to the objectives of the course. It does follow that students consider the objectives the most important part, and that is only natural since their evaluation is at stake. What teachers fail to see is that they can build many of the "magic moments" into their objectives. The activities in which they engage should result in learning. If they translate this learning into an objective, it does not follow that this is the only learning that will take place. The objectives contain those things to be learned which we consider most important in a course, but they cannot possibly contain all learning.

Closely associated with the teacher's fear of a loss of personal freedom is the fear of performance monitoring. To date few systems have been able to evaluate teachers effectively. In the last few years many schools have developed criteria for evaluating teachers, and some of these criteria are based upon student learning. Many teachers feel that by writing performance objectives they are driving nails into their own coffins. They want less—not more—monitoring. The future does not look auspicious for such points of view. Teacher salaries have risen, and taxpayers are demanding a measure of accountability. As was stated earlier, I feel it is better for teachers to define the measure of performance rather than to leave it to others to define. There is a second and valid fear, and that is that a set of performance objectives will be imposed upon them either from above or from outside. It is true that, if a teacher enters a system where the objectives have already been written, at least for the first year the teacher may have little input into the objectives. Nevertheless he can review the objectives and keep a notebook of the revisions that he wishes to see made when the appropriate time comes. Under normal circumstances, however, objectives should never be imposed. They should be reached by consensus, and teachers will have valid objections if they are not involved in the writing of these objectives. I do not foresee the imposition of sets of performance objectives by state or national mandate. I do foresee the development of state guidelines such as those being written in Michigan and Illinois. Both of these projects involve major expenditures of teacher time, and they should prove to be very helpful.

Another set of teacher objections centers around the student. Some teachers fear the imposition of one criterion of mastery for all students. They feel that some students will never be able to reach that level, and then they will have a problem as to whether or not to pass the student. There is also the problem of grading. What kind of grades does one assign if all students reach all the objectives? Many teachers object that the objectives are usually insignificant and that it is difficult to motivate students to study for the objectives. I suppose that most of these objections could be countered by suggesting that the teacher personalize the objectives. The student who cannot reach one mastery level is given a different objective or a different mastery level. All students should be graded on how well each achieves his own objectives. Teachers need to write objectives that are significant and to weed out those which are a waste of time. However, to personalize objectives the teacher needs a great quantity of lead time, and he needs to develop the skill and talent to diagnose, prescribe, and motivate the student to his highest potential.

There are also objections that center around the teacher as a person. First of all, there is the time involved. The teacher will have to give hours of his own time to develop the performance curriculum. He may have to compromise his own point of view in order to reach consensus; he may have to conform to a certain extent while teaching to the objectives established through compromise with his colleagues. While the ultimate emphasis may be on student learning, the teacher fears that the attention given to *his* part in the instructional act will be minimized. These are human concerns, and they lead many a teacher to deplore the use of performance objectives. The answers, as usual, lie in reason. There is no question as to the amount of preparation time involved, but schools can help teachers by giving them released time and by sponsoring salaried summer curriculum projects. The teacher will find that, while he may give up some of his own points of view, he will profit from the sharing of ideas, and his students will be in a better position if there is some scope and sequence to the curriculum. The difference between his future and past teaching will be that he has written down the important parts of his teaching. He will still have time for the "magic moments," and the teaching act will be as important as previously. Students may come to appreciate the teacher more when they are allowed to try alternate routes for reaching the objective.

So let us sum up the movement. It was born of the past; it has come into the present. At this time there are several factors which would seem to affect its chances for the future: the movement towards accountability, the mobility of the student population, the demand on the part of students for relevance, the open-access campus, the drop out and stop out movement, and the interest in individualized instruction. None of these factors was present the last time performance objectives were tried. What will be the future of performance objectives? Much depends on the success of the individualized instruction movement, although one can use objectives effectively without individualization. Much depends on the mandates of state educational offices. Much depends on the success of PPBS throughout the country. I think that the future will be propitious for performance objectives because I personally believe that individualization of instruction will increase. I believe that accountability will be mandated through legislation for public schools and possibly for universities, and that performance objectives will be around for some time to come.

Now for the most important question: will performance objectives humanize or dehumanize education? *This depends on the people who implement performance curricula.* They can and should humanize education if they are used judiciously. They will dehumanize education if they are imposed on teachers, if one set of objectives is demanded of everyone, if all students are expected to meet all objectives to an equal mastery level within the same time span (unless very minimal objectives are required), or if students are isolated from their teachers and their peers. In the final analysis, everything depends on one human being—the teacher. Only teachers can humanize or dehumanize education; no single movement or curricular development is capable of such an act. I have faith in teachers. If it can be demonstrated that the use of performance objectives will create a better teaching situation that will in turn help students to learn more effectively, I feel certain that teachers will accept and implement the idea. If this occurs, the movement will endure, and the improvement of education for all students will be the result.

REFERENCES

Allen, Edward D. "The Teacher as Catalyst: Motivation in the Classroom," in Frank Grittner, ed. *Student Motivation and the Foreign Language Teacher.* Skokie, Illinois: National Textbook Company, 1974, pp. 1-10.

Altman, Howard B., ed. *Individualizing the Foreign Language Classroom: Perspectives for Teachers.* Rowley, Massachusetts: Newbury House Publishers, 1972.

Belasco, Simon. "C'est la guerre? or Can Cognition and Verbal Behavior Co-exist in Second Language Learning?" in R. Lugton, ed. *Toward a Cognitive Approach in Second Language Acquisition.* Philadelphia: Chilton, 1972, pp. 191-230.

Bessell, Harold and Palomares, Uvaldo. *Methods in Human Development.* El Cajon: California, n.d.

Bloom, Benjamin S., ed. *Taxonomy of Educational Objectives: The Classification of Educational Goals, Handbook 1: Cognitive Domain.* New York: David McKay Company, 1956.

Brown, George Isaac. *Human Teachings for Human Learning: An Introduction to Confluent Education.* New York: Viking Press, 1971.

Clark, John L.D. "Measurement Implication of Recent Trends in Foreign Language Teaching," in Dale L. Lange and Charles James, eds. *Foreign Language Education: A Reappraisal.* The ACTFL Review of Foreign

Language Education, Vol. 4. Skokie, Illinois: National Textbook Company, 1972, pp. 219-57.

Disick, Renée. *Performance Objectives in Foreign Language Teaching.* MLS/Eric Focus Report 25. New York: MLA/Eric, 1971.

―――. "Teaching Toward Affective Goals in Foreign Language," Foreign Language Annals, 7 (1973) 95-101.

Duffy, E. James. "Directions for Learning–We Have the Tools," in *The 80's–Where Will the Schools Be?* Reston, Virginia: National Association of Secondary School Principals, 1974, pp. 4-8.

Grittner, Frank M. "Barbarians, Bandwagons and Foreign Language Scholarship," *The Modern Language Journal*, 57 (1973) 241-48.

―――. "Behavioral Objectives, Skinnerian Rats, and Trojan Horses," *Foreign Language Annals*, 6 (1972) 52-60.

Hoetker, James. "The Limitations and Advantages of Behavioral Objectives," *Foreign Language Annals*, 3 (1970) 560-65.

Hoyt, Kenneth B., *et al. Career Education: What It Is and How to Do It.* Salt Lake City: Olympics Publishing Company, 1972.

Jenks, C. L., Bostick, N., and Otto, J. G. *Education Management Program*, published by the Far West Laboratory for Educational Research and Development, 1972.

Krathwohl, David, Bloom, Benjamin, and Masia, Bertram B. *Taxonomy of Educational Objectives: The Classification of Educational Goals, Handbook II: Affective Domain*, New York: David McKay Company, 1964.

Lester, Kenneth A. and Tamarkin, Toby. "Career Education," in Gilbert A. Jarvis, ed. *Responding to New Realities.* The ACTFL Review of Foreign Language Education, Vol. 5. Skokie, Illinois: National Textbook Company, 1974, pp. 161-87.

Levy, Stephen L. "The Realities Facing the Profession," in Gilbert A. Jarvis, ed. *Responding to New Realities.* The ACTFL Review of Foreign Language Education, Vol. 5. Skokie, Illinois: National Textbook Company, 1974, pp. 9-36.

Mager, Robert. *Developing Attitude Toward Learning.* Palo Alto, California: Fearon Publishers, 1968.

―――. *Preparing Instructional Objectives.* Palo Alto, California: Fearon Publishers, 1962.

Nostrand, Howard L. "Empathy for a Second Culture: Motivations and Techniques," in Gilbert A. Jarvis, ed. *Responding to New Realities.* The ACTFL Review of Foreign Language, Vol. 5. Skokie, Illinois: National Textbook Company, 1974, pp. 263-327.

Popham, W. James, ed. *Criterion-Referenced Measurement*. Englewood Cliffs, New Jersey: Educational Technology Publications, 1971.

Reinert, Harry. "Beginners are Individuals, Too!" in Howard B. Altman, ed. *Individualizing the Foreign Language Classroom: Perspectives for Teachers*. Rowley, Massachusetts: Newbury House Publishers, 1972, pp. 89-101.

———. "Student Attitudes Toward Foreign Language—No Sale!" *Modern Language Journal*, 54 (1970) 107-12.

Seelye, H. Ned. "Performance Objectives for Teaching Cultural Concepts," *Foreign Language Annals*, 3 (1970) 107-12.

Silberman, Charles. *Crisis in the Classroom*. New York: Random House, 1970.

Simon, Sidney, Howe, Leland, and Kirschenbaum, Howard. *Values Clarification: A Handbook of Practical Strategies for Teachers and Students*. New York: Hart Publishing Company, 1972.

Steiner, Florence. "Behaviorial Objectives and Evaluation," in Dale L. Lange, ed. *Britannica Review of Foreign Language Education*, Vol. 2. Chicago: Encyclopaedia Britannica Educational Corporation, 1970, pp. 35-78.

———. "Performance Objectives in the Teaching of Foreign Languages," *Foreign Language Annals*, 3 (1970) 579-91.

———. "Sense and Nonsense in Foreign Language Textbooks," *Foreign Language Annals*, 7 (1973) 91-94.

Valdman, Albert. "Grammar and the Foreign Language Teacher," in Frank Grittner, ed. *Student Motivation and the Foreign Language Teacher*. Skokie, Illlinois: National Textbook Company, 1974, pp. 66-80.

Valette, Rebecca. *Directions in Foreign Language Testing*. New York: MLA/Eric, 1969.

Valette, Rebecca M. "Testing," in Emma M. Birkmaier, ed. *Britannica Review of Foreign Language Education*, Vol. 1., Chicago: Encyclopaedia Britannica Educational Corporation, 1969, pp. 343-74.

Vallette, Rebecca and Disick, Renée S. *Modern Language Performance Objectives and Individualization: A Handbook*. New York: Harcourt, Brace, Jovanovich, Inc., 1972.

Wilson, Virginia and Wattenmaker, Beverly. *Real Communication in Foreign Language*. Upper Jay, New York: Adirondack Mountain Humanistic Education Center, 1973.

INDEX

shifting emphasis to performance objectives, 10-11
teacher provides variety, 16
Seelye, H. Ned, 129, 135-136
Silberman, Charles, 5
Simon, Sid, 125
Sputnik, 72

Taxonomy, 2
Taxonomy, 51, 52-55:
  definition, 52
  and foreign language instruction, 53
  insuring connection of objectives and purposes, 54
  insuring variety, 54-55
  irrelevant to clarification of present teaching, 52
  and screening performance objectives, 53-54
Tennessee Foreign Language Association, 135
Testing, 56-62
  achievement, 57, 58
  American Association of Teachers of French, 61
  C.E.E.B. Achievement Tests, 61
  C.E.E.B. Advanced Placement Tests, 61
  comprehensive random achievement monitoring, 60
  criterion-referenced, 56, 57, 58, 69, 70
    construction, 60-61
    definition, 56-57
    differs from other tests, 57-58
    proper use, 58
    and specific performance objectives, 61
  designed before teaching, 59
  determined by teacher priorities, 58
  and foreign language teaching, 61-62
  improper uses, 56, 60-62
  and individualized education (*see* Individualized Education)
  Modern Language Achievement Tests, 61
  multiple choice:
    disadvantages, 59
  norm-referenced, 57-58, 62:
    best use of, 58
  Pimsleur Proficiency Tests, 61
  random sampling, 58
  by textbook authors, 58, 59, 61
  tied directly to performance objectives, 60, 61

(*see also* C.E.E.B.)
(*see also* Educational Testing Service)
Textbooks, 11, 15, 17, 18, 22, 129, 140, 151, 152-162:
  colleges, 160-162:
    differences in problems, 160
    factors to consider, 160
    geared to student needs, 160
    independent study, 161
    no language requirement, 160-161
    open admissions, 160
    performance objectives as guide, 160-161
    questions to ask, 161
    for upper level courses, 162
    variety of abilities, 161-162
  junior college, 157-159:
    explained to individual student, 159
    need for performance objectives, 158
    problems in selection, 157-158
    student needs, 158-159
    variety of objectives, 158-159
  secondary schools, 152-157:
    expanding set of objectives, 154-155
    funds, 156-157
    geared to specific students, 155
    and individualized education, 155-156
    order of materials, 155
    other factors in selection, 153
    P.P.B.S., 156
    performance objectives as guide, 153-156
    pilot program, 155
    problems of selection, 152-153
    sample questions to ask, 153-154
    select texts for review, 153
    written for "average" class, 18
Tyler, Ralph, 3

U.S. Office of Education, 168

Valdman, Albert, 99
Valette, Rebecca, 53
  and Disick, Renée, 53, 55, 56
Values clarification, 94, 125, 166
Verlaine, 108

Wattenmaker, Beverly, 125
Wilson, Virginia, 125
Writing (*see* Composition)